Good Beginnings

HIGH/SCOPE
EDUCATIONAL RESEARCH FOUNDATION
Ypsilanti, Michigan

Good Beginnings

Parenting in the Early Years

Judith Evans & Ellen Ilfeld

THE
HIGH/SCOPE
PRESS

Published by
THE HIGH/SCOPE PRESS
High/Scope Educational Research Foundation
600 North River Street
Ypsilanti, Michigan 48197
(313) 485-2000

Linda Eckel, Designer & Illustrator
Gary Easter, Photographer & Art Director

Library of Congress Cataloging in Publication Data

Evans, Judith
  Good beginnings

  Bibliography: p.
  Includes index.
  1. Parenting. 2. Infants (Newborn). 3. Infant
psychology. 4. Child development. I. Ilfeld, Ellen,
1955-   . II. Title
HQ755.8.E9   649'.122   82-885

ISBN 0-931114-15-2   AACR2

Printed in the United States of America.

Emergence. . .
In a room filled with masked strangers you entered this world.
Thru a haze of antiseptics I heard you cry out.
Child of my womb, fruit of my desire, you will be strong and beautiful
Healthy and secure.
You will reflect all that I do that is good.
I promise you will never want for anything.
I will stand at the gates of hell if it means saving you from the pain of total despair.
Now with the passing of time I see you growing away from me.
Is this where my importance ends?

No Mother, this is where I begin, separate from you. . .

At Second Sight: Pregnancy
The Theater Company of Ann Arbor

Contents

Preface

The information and suggestions in this book come from several sources. The theoretical underpinnings are to be found in the work of the psychologist Jean Piaget, who has spelled out in detail many of the intellectual changes children go through as they develop. He has described substages of cognitive growth within the "sensory-motor" stage which correspond to the first six stages we present. The seventh stage we discuss corresponds to the early part of the "preoperational" stage in Piaget's theory. A major difference between what Piaget describes and what we present is that Piaget's theory focuses only on cognitive development. In this book we present Piaget's description of cognitive functioning within the context of the young child's *total* development. This application of Piaget's theory has been derived from our work with parents and infants, home visitors, and community resource people in a succession of parent-infant education projects.

The High/Scope Foundation's work in parent-infant education began with the *Ypsilanti-Carnegie Infant Education Project* (1968-71), funded by the Carnegie Corporation of New York. In this program, professional staff visited the homes of local families with infants between the ages of three and eleven months. Meeting once weekly for sixteen months, the home visitor and parent would initiate activities with the baby, respond to games and other activities the baby initiated, and discuss child development, using the baby's actions as a focal point. Home visitors planned sessions together with parents, using a curriculum structured around Piagetian developmental theory, and sought to help parents see themselves as their infants' first and most important teacher. Results of evaluation have shown that those who participated in the program evidenced significantly more supportive verbal interaction with their children than did the comparison groups.

During the *Infant Videotaping Project* (1971-73), again funded by Carnegie, six families participated in a home visit program. Project staff again visited local homes to work with parents and infants, this time accompanied by a media crew that documented the unstaged activities and interactions on videotape. Using the resultant 270-hour library of tapes, High/Scope produced audio-visual programs on home visitor training, parent education, child development, and related subjects.

A third major parent-infant project, the consolidation of previous experience in a *Parent-to-Parent Model*, was supported in part by the Lilly Endowment and the National Institute for Mental Health. In this project, four women who had participated in one of the previous home visit programs conducted home visits themselves after being trained by High/Scope staff. The goal of the project was to prepare a complete training/delivery system for disseminating the home visit program to other sites. Fully implemented, the training/delivery system features a process whereby those who participate in home visits are, in turn, trained as home visitors; they conduct home visits and eventually train other parents. The Parent-to-Parent Model thus replicates itself within the local community, providing a strong framework for community service by and for parents.

Since 1978 we have been conducting a *Parent-to-Parent Dissemination Project*, funded by the Bernard van Leer Foundation of the Netherlands and by participating communities. For this project, the Parent-to-Parent Model with its training/delivery system is being implemented in a variety of communities.

The creation, operation, and evaluation of a succession of programs has shown that when we work with any parent population, we are dealing with a group of interested and vital people, each of whom brings to the program a unique set of skills and varying needs. This experience has reinforced our belief in the mutuality of roles between parents and program personnel; the focus is not on "eliminating deficits," but on the challenge of supporting and expanding present skills. Rather than use parents as an efficient means to get through to the infant, we view them as active, autonomous decision-makers for the infant and themselves.

This book is designed to encourage an informed decision-making process. Readers are helped to ask and answer questions about parenting from the standpoint of their own resources and the demands of their own situation. We have tried to be open enough in our descriptions that, regardless of family structure, social class, ethnic background, religious orientation, or work status, parents and other caregivers will find the book useful. Yet we are aware that some of what we say and suggest is clearly bound to certain social and ethnic cultures.

The diversity of people who will read and use this book is matched by the diversity of those who have contributed in some way to its development. We want to acknowledge several persons for their specific contributions, while recognizing that we have been influenced by countless others who personally and professionally are struggling with what it means to parent.

We thank Barbara Finberg and the Carnegie Corporation of New York for financial support and their belief in our earliest programs within which the seeds for the Parent-to-Parent Model, and this book, were sown.

We thank Barbara Reschly for her theoretical and practical insights into child development and for her continuous feedback on numerous ideas and drafts of the book.

We thank our colleagues—Sally Adler, Barbara Banet, Lois Bass, Nancy Brussolo, Ann Epstein, Mary Hohmann, Michelle Ludwig, and Fran Parker-Crawford for their information, anecdotes, reactions and thoughtful suggestions.

We thank Jackie Torres, Lori Murray, and Carol Ofiara for the hours and hours they spent typing drafts and more drafts of the manuscript.

We thank our editors, Charles Silverman and Lynn Spencer; our art director and photographer, Gary Easter; and our designer, Linda Eckel, for making this production special. We thank Carol Ofiara for the complicated typesetting of this book; and Dianne Kreis and Judy Clouse for their specialized contribution in preparing the pages for print.

And, with the deepest gratitude, we thank our own parents and children for what they have taught us about the challenges of parenting.

Good
Beginnings

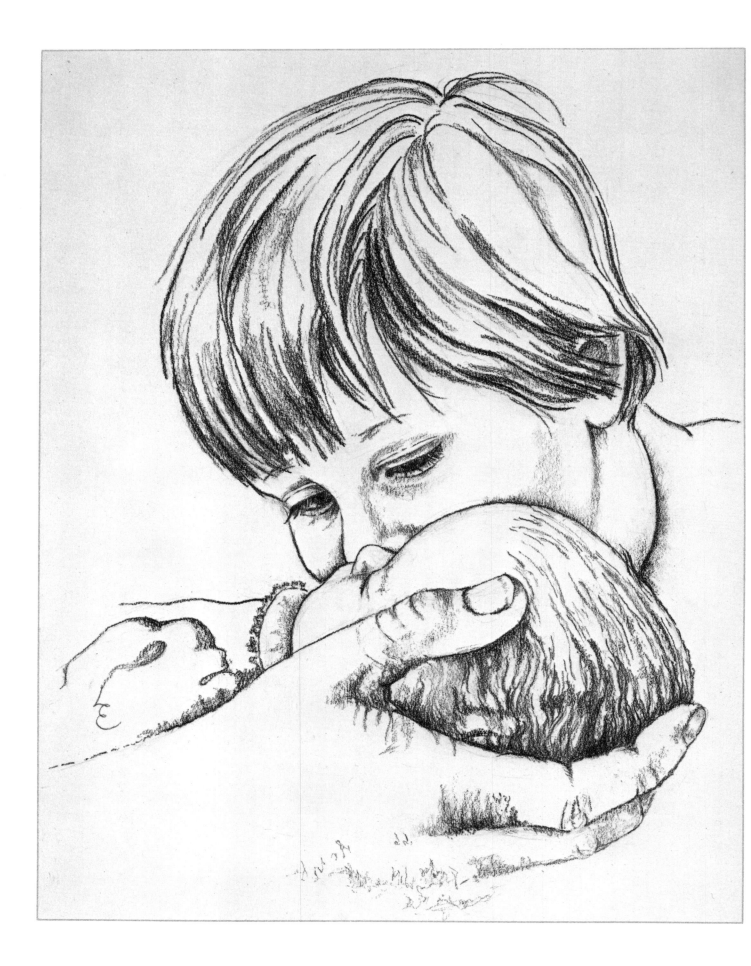

Chapter I

Introduction

Whether you've just had your first baby (or your fourth) or will be a significant part of an infant's life as a caregiver, this book can help you examine your parenting skills. But we aren't in the business of giving "right" answers. When it comes to human babies—and human caregivers—there just *isn't* one set of right answers. Each situation offers you a choice. The more information you have, the more able you will be to choose what's best for you and the baby.

Consider what you already know about raising children. *If the baby begins to cry, what do you do?* Experienced parents probably have many definite ideas about why the baby is crying. But even new parents will have some strategies. You might try rocking the baby—something you've seen mothers do in the park. You might check to see if the baby is wet—an idea picked up from diaper commercials. Even when you can't think of a single solution to a problem, you can probably think of someone to call and ask—your own mother, a friend, a nurse, a neighbor. There are few situations in which you will be helpless.

Why, then, use a book on "parenting" at all? After all, each of us was a child, and most of us know at least what we *don't* want to do. But the job of parenting is more complicated than it was in the past. Most of us are no longer living with our extended family—with parents, grandparents, aunts and uncles on hand to give us advice. The old values that once were straightforward for many of us have changed; cultures are mixing, strict sex-role separation is no longer desirable, economic and social conditions encourage mothers to have jobs outside the home, and the pace of life is quicker than it used to be. There are more conflicting influences on both you and the child than ever before. Today, not only do you have to *play* the role of parent, you have to *define* it as well.

What does being a parent mean? How does it fit in with the rest of your life? What do you expect for and from your family? You will probably have to ask yourself these questions many times over during the next several years. Being a parent introduces many changes in your life that can make you feel overwhelmed or trapped. Suddenly you can't come and go as you please. Every little errand or task requires planning and forethought, and you are thrown into the great babysitter scramble. Your relationships with other adults can be thrown off balance or distanced. Your sleep may be constantly disrupted, leaving you as tired as if you'd been doing hard physical labor all day. You may find yourself acting as cranky and whiney and "unreasonable" as your child.

Learning to be a parent means, in part, learning to look ahead and anticipate the baby's needs. *What are the needs of an infant?* If you can't answer this question off the top of your head, don't worry, many caregivers can't. Your infant will give you many cues about what she needs. As you learn to read these cues, you will feel more secure about what to do with and for her. You can also get information about what infants need from other sources—from your doctor, from your parents or friends who are parents, from books and articles. This book will describe for you the kinds of things you might expect as your infant grows and changes. It will suggest some of the questions you might need to consider; occasionally it will offer advice. But you will have to identify your own parenting skills as you go along. You will have to learn when to use trial and error, when to call on experts (your doctor, other parents), and when to wait and let time answer your questions. Just as children grow and develop, so do parents. Whatever else parenting is, it is a continual series of adjustments to continually changing demands. As soon as you have adjusted to your crawling infant, for example, she turns into a toddler. These constant changes can

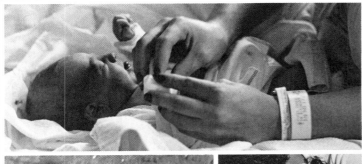

As infants grow they gain new abilities which make them "new persons." At each of these stages they require some new kinds of parenting.

leave you perplexed and frustrated, but once you have identified the new problem and figured out some new approaches and one of them works, you'll feel exhilarated. You will take great pride in your child's development, but you should also take great pride in yourself and your own developing ability to solve the problems of raising a child.

In the chapters that follow, we describe the infant as she goes through the stages of growth during the first three years of life. Each child grows at her own rate and has some character traits that stand out more than others. Within the limits of normal growth and development, each child will seem to grow quickly in some areas and slowly in others. It doesn't make sense to describe children according to strict age charts. Instead, we focus on the stages of development that are characteristic of most young children and describe each stage in some detail. In our work with parents and infants, we have observed and identified seven stages: **Heads Up** (0-1 month), **Looker** (approximately 1-4 months), **Creeper-Crawler** (approximately 4-8 months), **Cruiser** (approximately 8-12 months), **Walker** (approximately 12-18 months), **Doer** (approximately 18-24 months), and **Tester** (approximately 24-36 months). While each stage includes a general age level, the best way to identify which stage your child is in is by observing her. This book can serve as an observation guide.

We also suggest activities you can do with your child as she grows. These activities are not meant to be lessons but rather ways of discovering, observing, appreciating, and enjoying to the fullest all the new skills your child is developing. The more experience your child has with each new skill and concept, the better her base will be for future learning. Her muscles and her understanding of the world both need exercise! And the more you enjoy her learning process the more *she* will.

There is a wealth of information available for you today about children and their needs, but wading through it is a big job, and sorting out the opinions of experts can seem an impossible task. We offer this book in the hope that it will help you to become an expert yourself—the foremost expert on your own child.

Ways to Use This Book

Before the baby is born. Many parents find they have more time to read before the baby arrives. While you won't remember everything you read, you will get a feeling for what the book has to offer and how you might use it later on. Reading before the brith will also help you prepare for those first days and weeks, which are probably your most immediate concern.

Crisis by crisis. This is when that first reading and the index come in handy. Perhaps bathtime frightens rather than delights your newborn infant. You look in the index under "Bathtime," page 21, and turn to that section for immediate suggestions and strategies.

Problem-solving at the end of the day. Many parents find it helpful to sit down together for a few minutes after the baby is settled at the end of

the day to review the day's triumphs and disasters. This book can be used at these times as a resource for planning. You might ask such questions as, "What can we do tommorrow to support and encourage Tommy's discovery that he can reach for and get the toys in his crib?" or "If Tommy dumps his cereal on the floor again I'm going to scream. What can I do differently tomorrow at breakfast time?" What you plan may may not be entirely successful, but using this book as an observation and planning tool will give you a way to actively participate in your child's development.

Our goal is: 1) to help you observe your child, and 2) to help you turn that knowledge into action.

Keeping a diary. In the companion volume, *Good Beginnings: A Baby's Diary from Conception to Age Three,* you can write down your experiences, feelings, thoughts and observations and save them for you and your child. The diary can serve as a record of your experience before your child is born—the books you read, who you first tell you are pregnant and their reaction, the advice you get from family, friends and neighbors, the questions you ask the doctor and the responses you get, the medicines you take during pregnancy, the names you choose and discard, the infant's delivery—all the things that fill your time and thoughts and affect your moods as you are waiting and preparing for the child to enter your life. Once the child is born you can record what your child is doing at each stage of development, problems you encounter, issues you discuss with other parents, your own feelings about parenting, your family's responses to its newest member, and who and what is helpful along the way.

As a parent you are so intensely caught up in the present that the past quickly fades. You are so busy keeping up with your toddler you can barely recall that she once slept most of the day and you worried that you would never get a chance to play with her! As you read through it many years hence, the diary will help you remember the reality of raising a child and can become a real part of the child's history.

How This Book Is Organized

Parents often marvel at the distinct ways their children expressed themselves when they were born. Each person's character and personality are indeed distinct, are in fact *unique,* because they represent a unique combination of inborn temperament and mental and physical responses to the world. We have identified five elements of children's mental and physical responses to the world. These elements work together to determine the quality and nature of the child's growth. They are (1) the child's physical abilities; (2) the child's understanding of the physical world; (3) the child's sense of self; (4) the child's relationships with other people; and (5) the child's ability to communicate thoughts, wishes, needs, and feelings. Each chapter in this book is organized around these elements but the order in which the elements are presented varies due to their relative importance at each developmental stage. Since each chapter is concerned with one of the stages of growth that we have identified, you will be able to follow your infant's development *systematically.* At the same time, because of the knowledge you will gain through guided observation, you'll be creating the supportive environment that is so important to your child's development.

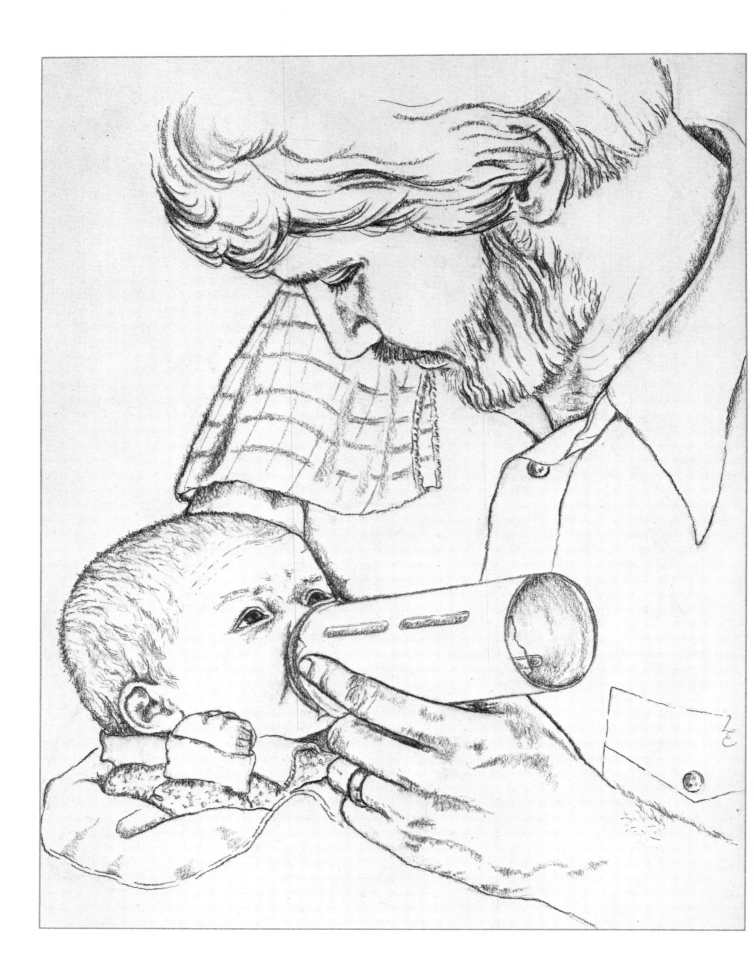

Chapter II

Heads Up

Right in the delivery room, the newborn infant has an immediate reaction to the environment. There are as many reactions as there are infants: vibrant, stunned, fearful, raging, quiet, disturbed, peaceful. Most of the child's first hours of life are spent adjusting physically to the world around her. Her breathing mechanism starts up, often aided by crying. She must clear her lungs of the phlegm which filled them in the womb. She must adjust to the temperature changes of the delivery room, to the physical battering her body received during the birth, and to the lights and sounds around her.

No matter how many children they have had, usually the first thing parents of a new baby ask is, IS THE BABY O.K.? For different parents this means different things. Is her body all there? Is she healthy? Is she going to be a normal child? The questions hide all the fears you have, all the fantasies about who this person is going to be, as well as all the feelings of powerlessness.

Many things you do before the birth help assure that the baby is indeed O.K. The more you know about the process the better. Before the delivery you have to make some choices that will set the scene for the infant's arrival:

• Where will the baby be born? What are the rules and routines there?

• Will a sedative be used? If so, what kind? How does it make you feel when you come out of it?

• If a Caesarean is necessary, who will approve it, and under what conditions?

• Will the father or others be present at the birth? Afterward?

• If it's a boy, will he be circumcised?

Other people make choices during the birth. The attendant makes judgments about the progress of labor, and may adjust plans for your safety and the child's. Everyone involved—you, the attendants, the baby herself—must be prepared to handle anything out of the ordinary. The baby has remarkable reflexes for accomplishing this. The attendant generally has thorough training and special equipment. You, too, should be as well informed as possible.

You may be surprised at the appearance of your new baby. She is probably messy and slimy. Often she is covered with a dark down (which will disappear after a few weeks). She is usually wrinkled, and her features may be squashed to one side, or battered from the birth.

After the birth, the infant is usually placed on the mother's stomach. Some attendants do this because it makes cutting the cord easier; others do it because they believe it's important for the mother and child emotionally. Some babies begin to breathe on their own, others must be aided by a pat on the bottom or by being suspended upside down or by the use of special equipment. The baby's own system helps in this process. She often cries, which brings air into her lungs. She gags and

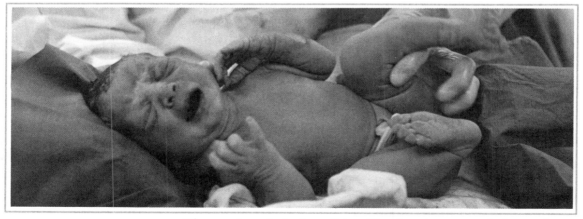

The newborn baby is nothing like the pictures on baby products!

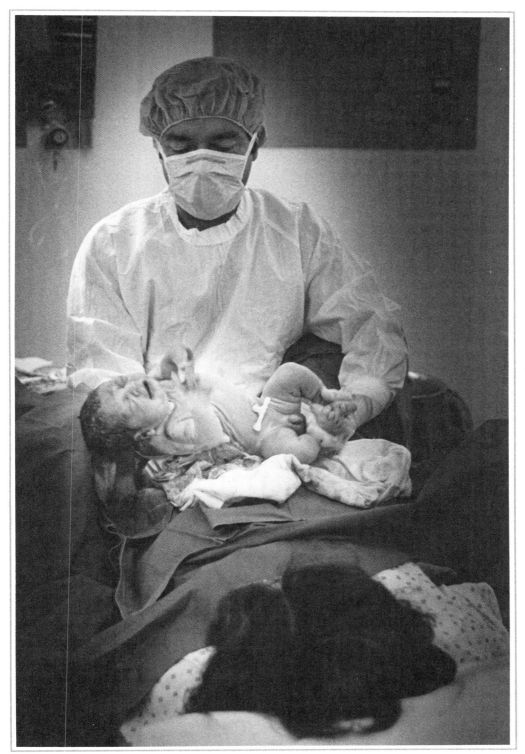

Talk with your doctor and others familiar with the delivery process. Keep asking questions until you feel satisfied you have the answers you need. Also, talk with other new parents. What did they go through? What is it really like?

coughs to help remove the phlegm, and she squirms, which causes her blood to circulate more vigorously. There is great variation in these responses from infant to infant; they are often the stamp of an infant's temperament.

The first meeting is not, however, a clear and uncomplicated introduction of parents to infant. You have been through an exhausting experience. The infant may be affected by sedatives you have been given or stress you have gone through. You may be groggy or experiencing anything from elation to disappointment to relief, or some combination of all these feelings. The infant may have physical difficulties to contend with: getting her breathing started, being startled by sounds and bright lights. You may be distracted by worries and by the confusion around you.

The infant is a separate being now, with a system all her own, and with a new set of needs. Many of the initial needs of a newborn are taken care of by those attending the birth. The attendants check the baby's eyes for responsiveness and often administer eyedrops to protect them from disease. They check reflexes, count toes and fingers, check the pulse, and

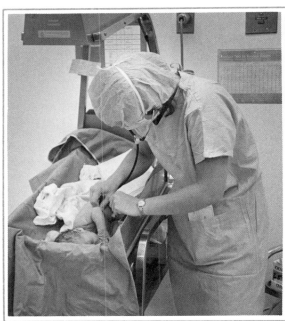 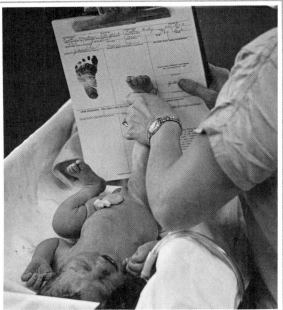

finally swaddle the baby to protect her from the cold. Once the infant's needs are taken care of, you may be moved into the recovery room, and the baby either accompanies you or is removed to a nursery.

If you and the infant are together in the same room during the hospital stay, you have a chance to get acquainted on your own schedule. But if you're in a situation where the infant is only with you for short periods of time each day, you'll have to get to know her within limits which may not match your mood or hers. This may make it more difficult to get acquainted, but you'll still have many opportunities to find out more about this new person.

Explore your baby physically. Examine the toes and the tiny fingernails; watch the changes of skin color. Try holding the infant in various positions to see which is most comfortable and to get used to the feel of her. Don't be afraid to ask questions of nurses, doctors, friends, relatives, and other mothers.

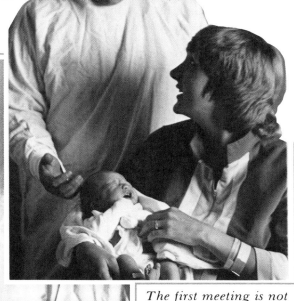

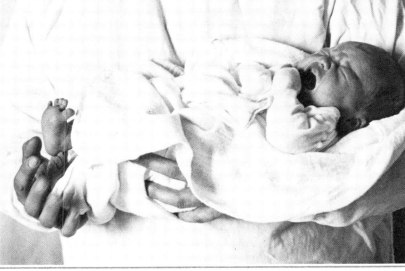

The first meeting is not a clear and uncomplicated introduction of parents to infant. You have all been through an exhausting experience. The infant may be affected by sedatives you have been given or stress you have gone through. You may be groggy or experiencing anything from elation to disappointment to relief, or some combination of all these feelings.

It will probably take you a while to learn how to console her, and to recognize how she reacts to various situations—being hungry, being naked, being fed, hearing sudden noises. Each infant has her own responses, her own pattern, so you'll need to watch your baby carefully to understand hers. How quickly does she calm down when comforted, or when left on her own for a while?

Right from the start a bond is being formed between you and your infant.

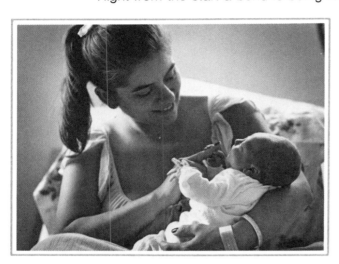

Every contact you have with the infant is an opportunity to get to know her. When she is calm and attentive you can gaze at her, catch her eye. She can begin to get used to your face and voice. You can hold her, move her gently, make sounds, watch her, speak to her. Learn to recognize how she responds to you. Does she lie very still or squirm about? Does your voice calm her or excite her? How easy is it to catch her gaze? to keep it?

Sense of Self
Beginnings

Chris came crying into the hands of the doctor. He continued crying while on his mother's stomach and during the cleaning, checking, and swaddling procedures. When handed to his father, who patted and jostled him gently, he stopped, opened his eyes, and began making sucking sounds and motions.

Infants make their personality obvious right from the beginning. They shout their way into the world or arrive without a complaint. They recover immediately from the strains of birth or take their time and develop one "complication" after another. They move about restlessly or seem to be intently watching. They cry and fret or coo and smile. Usually, they do a unique combination of all these things. As with any person, the baby's sense of self will affect not only what she can and can't do within a given situation, but the *way* she does things.

The Physical Environment

It's important to recognize how the physical environment is affecting you and your infant. In the hospital you may feel nervous in unfamiliar surroundings. It may be hard to relax and get to know your baby with other people watching and with the time limits many hospitals impose. You may feel disoriented by the routine you are expected to follow. You may feel inexperienced compared with the hospital staff, who deal with hundreds of infants each month. Whatever you are feeling, it is important to recognize it and to discuss it with people who can support you.

The infant, too, is reacting to his environment. The bright lights and noises of a hospital are usually designed more for the convenience of adults than newborn infants. The crying of other babies in the nursery and the feeding and changing schedule (which follows a clock rather than the infant's demands) can cause tension which even the most skillful of mothers might not be able to relieve.

Be prepared for less than perfect conditions (every arrangement, even home birth, will require adjustments), and try to do what you can to make yourself and your child comfortable. You may find that the major thing which concerns you is something no one ever mentioned: you hate the wallpaper in your room; you resent the tone of voice people use with you; you don't want visitors, not even the baby's father. These reactions are natural: having a baby is a very emotional and personal experience, most hospitals and childbirth settings are quite impersonal. You may well feel there's something terribly wrong with you. There isn't! Your body is going through many changes that affect how you feel about yourself. A new person has entered your life, and that upsets the way you have been living. Give yourself time to adjust to these changes.

Once the baby is home, you are in more familiar territory, but this can cause new problems. You may miss the expert help of hospital staff and the "pampering" of staying in bed and having people wait on you. The infant is suddenly yours full-time, and you have to figure out how much to hold him, where to put him, when to feed him and take care of him, and how to get the rest you need. Being home can remind you of all the work you're not getting done and probably won't get done for a while. Other family members may not know how to react to the demands and schedule of an infant and may make your task more difficult. It helps if everyone shares the work and discusses what the baby and each family member needs.

The infant should have a relatively calm atmosphere. Loud noises and bright lights can cause him to "startle"—a physical reaction in which he tenses suddenly, arches his back, and throws his arms out; this is very disquieting and can keep the baby agitated. Of course it isn't possible to create the perfect environment, with just the right amount of calm and quiet, but happily, infants are adaptable people. Take a look at where the baby will be sleeping, eating, bathing, playing. Will these spaces meet his needs? Will they also allow other people in the household to meet their own needs? If you can answer in the affirmative, you will have a good chance of making the adjustment as smooth as possible.

Physical Abilities
Basics

When Josh was born his mother was worried because her milk didn't come down right away. She did not realize that the liquid (colostrum) he was getting from her was providing him with important antibodies, nor that the colostrum was more easily digested than her breast milk. His mother feared that he was starving and when he began to lose weight she panicked and asked the nurse for a bottle. The mother would have been more confident if she had known that Josh would "naturally" lose weight and that his body needed and expected this adjustment period.

The more you know about what the infant needs, the more you can be at ease with her. The infant's physical needs take up much of your time during the first month. She often appears to sleep and eat and not much else. Because of this, she appears to be completely helpless and dependent. But a newborn's body has several built-in abilities which not only help her survive, but support her growth. During the first several days, before a mother's milk has come down, the baby is able to survive on fat and tissue built up before birth. A special "rooting" reflex causes the infant to turn her head to seek the breast, and a "sucking" reflex causes the infant to fasten on and suck automatically. The infant will suck, not because she's starving but because she is "programmed" to respond this way. When her body needs food, she has a way of getting it.

Grasping is another reflex in the newborn. Try placing your finger in the infant's hand for her to grasp! At this early age, the infant's grasp is so strong she can be pulled to a sitting position. But she is not aware that she is holding on, so you need to support her with your other hand because she may let go.

Because your infant looks so helpless, you will probably worry about many things. One common worry is that the baby will suffocate. This is not impossible, but the baby is born with a protective response to prevent this from happening. When placed on her stomach, she will raise her head away from anything blocking her nose and mouth. At the very beginning this is a reflex, something her muscles do automatically. But within a few weeks the baby learns to control this ability, to lift her head on purpose. This is more than a protection— once she learns to turn her head, she is able to see more.

The smile is also a reflex at first. It is the infant's natural expression of pleasure, and sometimes of discomfort. By the end of the first month or so the infant is able to control this ability and to smile when she is pleased. But a truly "social smile" doesn't come until the next stage.

The infant's eyes cannot focus on an object less than eight or more than twelve inches away. But she's able to follow a slowly moving object with her eyes if it is moved within her range of vision. (You may have to hold it in one place for quite a while before she "finds" it.) If the infant focuses on an object and it is moved too quickly, she won't be able to follow it. Only gradually is she able to follow objects moved more rapidly and to remain interested in them for longer periods of time.

The infant's other senses are also developing. Sudden or sharp noises will cause her to "startle." After a few experiences with a sharp sound, an infant will become accustomed to it and cease to startle; this shows her emerging ability to learn from experience. Music and other soft sounds seem to soothe her. From early on you can see an infant moving in response to the rhythms in adult speech and often responding with a smile.

Touch is important to an infant, and an important way for adults to communicate with her. Often if you rub the infant gently around her mouth (her most sensitive area), she will calm down and cease crying. Touching the infant lightly on her stomach, blowing softly on her skin, and caressing the palms of her hands and soles of her feet are ways to communicate with her and to give her sensual experiences.

Feeding, Diapering, Bathing

During this first month of life, activities with or for the baby are mostly things you can do during the times when you feed, diaper, and bathe him, or during the time he is awake by himself. Once you have an idea of some of the things that are happening during these times, it is easier to see ways in which you can help your infant develop new skills.

Feeding. When feeding your infant, there are many questions to consider. The first one for most mothers is, the bottle or the breast (or some combination of both)? Regardless of which choice you make, there are other aspects of feeding you should also consider.

In what setting (room, position of mother and child, degree of seclusion from others) *should the feeding take place?* It would be ideal, of course, if there were a quiet place to feed the baby, with no other interruptions or demands on you. This isn't always possible. Often there are other children in the household, or space is limited, or household tasks need to be done. Consider what place is available to you that would be relatively free of distractions (lights, sounds, other people, pets). Try it out for a while and see how your baby reacts. Try out various positions also (lying down, sitting in a chair, holding the baby "football" fashion under one arm—whatever still allows you to cuddle him). Some infants are extremely sensitive to all these factors and others aren't.

Three-year-old Paul was jealous of his mother's feeding times with his new brother. Whenever he noticed his mother getting ready to feed the baby, he would run up and down the hall, screaming. His mother found that if she had him sit next to her on the couch with his favorite book, he was much more pleased when feeding time came around.

If there are other children causing distractions, set up activities they can do while you are feeding the infant. Provide them with something which will keep them from feeling excluded but also keep them from disrupting the infant's feeding time. You may actually find that during daytime feedings most of your energies are focused not on the baby himself but on creating a peaceable atmosphere in which he can eat. Don't worry that you are neglecting him. You are probably doing the best thing for him by keeping his older brothers and sisters content at this time. You can then use the evening and nighttime feedings to concentrate more exclusively on him.

How long should feedings take and how frequently should they occur? Generally, when the infant is hungry, he will let you know. But many parents and caregivers have other schedules which they must also take into account when setting up a feeding routine. For example, a mother who works outside the home may have to schedule regular breaks when she will feed her child.

In the first month a baby gets hungry frequently, every two to five hours, and two or three times during the night. How long the feeding takes will vary from baby to baby; it needs to be worked out between you and your infant. Be suspicious of anyone suggesting rigid feeding schedules—infants have their own feeding rhythm, which must be taken into account.

Given a chance, the infant will establish his own feeding pattern. This pattern may not be at convenient intervals for you— especially those nighttime feedings which come just when you are falling asleep. But, generally, by the time the infant is five weeks old, he will only cry for one middle-of-the-night feeding.

If there are problems with the feeding situation—if the infant seems cranky and dissatisfied—then it is time to look at what is happening. Is the infant taking in too much air, eating too quickly, unusually slowly? Does he lose the nipple, fret, react passively? Is he distracted by lights or sounds, other people, your actions? To what extent is he affected by your mood, your ability to attend to him?

Because an infant needs security, feeding time needs to be a reassuring time for him. If he has trouble, try to find ways to help him out. Some babies need frequent burping because they take in too much air. All babies need cuddling, though too much can be a distraction for some. It's good to talk or sing or croon to a baby, but if this keeps him from eating, limit it to pauses in feeding. Try stroking

his cheek, his hand, or the sole of his foot. If an infant has trouble holding the nipple, perhaps another position would help him, or a supportive hand.

Sometimes an infant will eat too quickly and will need help in slowing down. In these cases, a certain amount of distraction for the infant can be a good thing. Other infants seem to be distracted frequently and need help getting back to feeding; feeding in a slightly darkened room may help. If the infant is having trouble staying awake, perhaps he is not yet hungry and was fretting to be held rather than fed. Babies do signal their needs, but it is possible to misread the signals. Finally, if the baby is having trouble eating and this seems to relate to your mood, do whatever you can to relax and enjoy the feeding. Remember, you are an important part of the feeding routine and deserve consideration, too.

How much nourishment will the infant need and how can you be sure he is getting it? Your doctor or healthcare worker will be able to give you information on this. But also trust your instincts. If your baby is taking longer to eat than the guidelines say, or if he is still hungry after feeding, pay attention to his crying and sucking patterns. It's possible that his suck is not very strong yet, or that he has an unusually big appetite. If he consistently eats a large amount and then throws it up, perhaps he is eating too quickly, or is continuing to eat because of the pleasure of being at the breast or bottle. Discussion with your doctor of the baby's particular habits and needs will go a long way toward reassuring you and creating a good feeding situation.

Feeding time is a time for you and your infant to establish bonds. It is an intimate time, physically and emotionally. By holding and cuddling your baby (whether you are using a bottle or the breast) and communicating with him, you are giving him warmth, which helps him develop trust and a sense of security.

Feeding time can be a cuddling-and-being-together time. Catch your baby's eye; return his gaze. Watch him to see what you can notice about him. What movements does he tend to make? Which parts of his body does he use most often? How does he react to noises, lights, other people? What does he look at while feeding and while being held? How does he react when you talk to him, or sing? What sounds does he make? How does he react when you make faces at him or when you imitate his facial expressions? Give him your finger to grasp. If you are bottle-feeding, let him watch the bottle as you move it slowly from side to side.

Diapering. When you are changing your infant's diapers, you have a good opportunity to interact with him. You will probably be taught procedures for diapering in the hospital, and will have made the decision about the kind of diapers and laundering method to use. What they might not teach you in the hospital is all the emotional elements of the diapering time. How does your baby react to the position you place him in? Some babies startle when they are placed on their back. Others feel abandoned or en-

dangered physically when unclothed. Try keeping one hand on the infant's stomach to let him know you're there.

How does your baby react to being changed? Is he alert? Is he sleepy and unaware of your actions? If he is playful, there are many things you can do with him. Many infants enjoy being patted and rubbed. Try blowing on his tummy, smiling at him, making sounds. If you can catch his eye, help him strengthen his "looking" ability by moving your head slowly enough that he can follow it.

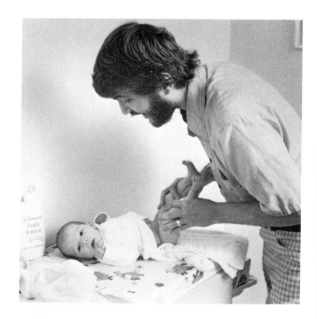

Changing time is a good time to give your baby some exercise. Many infants will "bicycle" with their legs or move their arms and legs randomly. You can join them in this by holding their feet and helping them cycle. You can contribute sound-effects. Lift the infant's legs and let them fall, or push on his feet gently. You can exercise the infant's arms by stretching them out and bringing them back to center. If he appears to enjoy it, you can continue as long as he wants. Often the baby will grasp your finger, and you can pull him carefully to a sitting position; while this can be fun, it does *not* help to develop the ability to sit at this early age; be sure to support his head with your other hand.

If the infant cries inconsolably during changing time, check to make sure he isn't lying on something uncomfortable or being poked by a pin. Has his body color changed much? Many babies are extremely sensitive to temperature changes and will let you know by crying.

Bathing. Bathtime can easily become war time if you're not especially careful about the baby's feelings and signals. Some infants are frightened by the unusual sensations and need reassurance. To approach the bath only with the idea that "it's good for you" is not helpful. Bathtime is an especially important time to work on developing in your infant a sense of trust. Again, while you may be taught the basics of bathing in a childcare course, it's important to consider your own infant's individual needs. For many infants, "restriction" (such as having a diaper over them while in the bath) is a reassurance. Other infants demonstrate a desire to be free of restrictions; they may flail their arms and legs, making it hard to hold onto them.

You may want to include brothers and sisters at bathtime. Some siblings, for example, enjoy washing their dolls while you wash the baby, while other siblings may feel important using a special wash mitt to help you wash the new brother or sister. They will probably also enjoy mopping up the floor afterwards.

For many infants bathtime is a delight. Your infant may enjoy kicking, splashing, making noises, having warm water slowly poured over his body, or being gently rubbed. Try imitating his noises. Talk, sound-effects, and smiling are all important ways to reassure the baby that he is safe and secure and can enjoy the new sensations he is feeling.

Many infants enjoy playing while un-clothed before or after bathtime. The free-

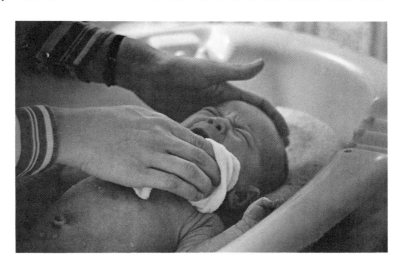

dom from restriction gives them a chance to exercise and play. It gives you a chance to communicate with your baby by touch. Make sure that if the baby is unwrapped, he is not exposed to excessive cold. With today's energy-saving temperatures, infants often need some extra protection.

Relationships
Building trust

During the first month you will learn not only what your baby's responses are, but how intense they are and how frequent. You'll learn to adjust your actions to suit her responses and learn which responses work with her. You'll provide physical care, emotional care, interesting experiences. The infant needs all of these to thrive. Her body is growing and requires support—she needs to be fed, changed, burped, and rocked to sleep. Her intellect, senses, and emotions are developing; they are supported when she is being cuddled, held,

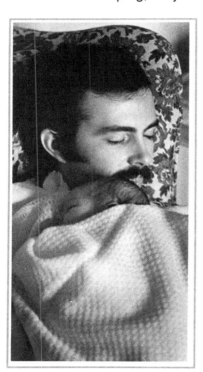

spoken to, touched, played with—all of which lead to a feeling of security. It is up to the people in the baby's world to provide security.

It is crucial to the baby's health, both physical and mental, that you develop a supportive, trusting relationship with her. This requires give and take. She will respond to you and cause you to respond to her with her crying and cooing and with her eyes and body movement. And you, too, will both respond to her and seek her response.

It may not be obvious to you that the infant is "receiving" your communications. But if the seemingly random motions which the infant produces when you are talking were filmed and played back at a slower rate, it would be possible to see that her own movements reflect the rhythm of your speech patterns. The infant is learning how to respond to the people she knows in the ways her body will allow.

During the first month of life, the infant learns to recognize the person who is her primary caregiver. Generally, this is the mother, but it may not be. (In cases where two people take care of her equally, the infant can learn to recognize both.) She responds to your voice and will look at you intently. When presented with strangers, the infant will look away fairly quickly, but with people she knows, she will continue her gaze. She is more likely to respond with body movements when you are talking than when strangers are talking. Also, the infant responds to your cuddling by snuggling into you; with a stranger she will tend to be stiffer, and her body will give less.

Some infants do not give very clear signals to adults. They may seem unresponsive, may fret constantly, or may appear to be uninterested in communicating. If this is the case, it is important to watch carefully to make sure you aren't missing something. Is there any change or reaction when you speak to your infant, cuddle her, feed her? Some infants show pleasure by smiling and waving their arms. Others show it by becoming very still. If your infant is not very outgoing, you'll probably have to spend more time and effort "conversing" with her. You may also have to remind yourself at times to respond to her, because whatever her personality, she will need warm, loving, and supportive contact with you in order to grow and develop.

You & Your Baby's Learning

What does your baby learn during the first few years?

- He becomes aware of his body and its parts. He learns to use his body.
- He learns where he ends and you begin.
- He learns to perceive and respond to a variety of sensations—smells, sights, sounds, textures.
- He becomes familiar with the people around him and learns many ways of communicating with them.
- He gains an awareness of objects and a gradual understanding of how they work and what effects his actions have on them.

What is your role in your infant's learning?

- You are the go-between for your baby and his environment.
- You are a provider—of stimulation to catch his interest, of responses to his attempts to communicate, and of physical care.
- You are a protector—you keep him safe and limit his environment so he can feel in control of himself.
- You help him to achieve what he sets out to do.

In all, you are his First Important Person. It's from you that he learns to trust, to get comfort, to communicate, and to respond to the world around him.

Crying and Soothing

Since crying is one of the most stressful things you will have to contend with in these early months, it's important to discuss what causes the infant to cry and to describe some ways to soothe him. One of the most common reasons for crying is hunger. The infant is simply ready to eat, so he cries. While sucking is soothing for the infant, to satisfy hunger his stomach needs to be full.

A second cause of crying is changes in temperature. An infant is most likely to be content when his body temperature is about ninety degrees. Warm babies tend to sleep more deeply. If they are colder, they are in a lighter state of sleep and thus are more easily awakened. A wet diaper in itself is not something the infant would respond to by crying, but it may cool him down and for this reason make him cry.

Another thing that can make a baby cry is being unclothed. Many infants are uncomfortable when they feel exposed. Soothing the infant when this happens may take more than putting a towel or blanket over him; he may need to be swaddled or have close contact with you.

Some infants simply cry during a regular time of day, most frequently in the evening. While this crying may be associated with pain, it is very difficult to tell. The best thing to do is to try soothing the infant when the crying begins; if the soothing doesn't work, you may have to let him cry it out (which he may do for half an hour or more), trying to soothe him now and then. The child will outgrow this crying, so don't despair.

Crying may be caused by a sudden change in the environment: a loud noise, a very bright light, being thrown off balance. The infant can usually be soothed rapidly in these situations if you cuddle him and reassure him with your voice and touch that everything is all right.

We suggest three ways you can soothe a crying infant during the first few months. One is to provide a repeated rhythm. You can rock the child, take him for a ride in a stroller or the car, or put him in an automatic swing. You can provide musical rhythm in the background—this can be a radio playing or you singing; frequently this will soothe the child to sleep. Don't be afraid to experiment. One father whose son cried regularly for at least an hour each evening pulled out his harmonica and began to play the only harmonica tune he knew. The baby quieted down and remained quiet as long as he could hear the harmonica. Eventually his eyes would close and he'd sleep peacefully until his next feeding.

A second way to soothe the infant is to keep him from making himself cry. This may sound strange, but one of the things that happens as the infant begins to cry is that his crying causes him to cry more. The crying itself distresses the infant, and the thrashing of his arms and legs as he cries gets his whole body going. What you can do is help him unwind so he's no longer stimulating himself. This is where swaddling (wrapping snugly in a blanket) comes in. What swaddling does is restrict the child; it

holds him in, gives him a firm sense of limits, and provides security. To swaddle the child completely may not be necessary: for some children it is enough to lay them on their stomach, hold their bottom firmly, and rub or pat their back; others are soothed if you rub their stomach while they are on their back. All of these actions limit the infant's ability to stimulate himself.

A third way to calm infants is to let them soothe themselves. Sucking is one of the self-soothing techniques an infant uses. Some people have found that pacifiers are helpful since they give the infant a chance to suck without being overfed. If your baby does depend on a pacifier for comfort, be sure to keep at least two "spares" on hand because,

unlike thumbs, pacifiers have a distinct tendency to fall in the dirt, to disappear altogether, and eventually, with the advent of teeth, to disintegrate.

Children who use pacifiers instead of their thumbs are not likely to give them up until they are two or three years old. One little boy observed with some astonishment just before his third birthday that his two-year-old friend, Gretchen, didn't have a "binky," as he called his pacifier. "Dear Gretchen," he dictated to his mom, "here is my binky. It is for you. I don't need it because I am big now."

Another object the child may begin to suck is his own thumb. Some infants begin thumbsucking in the womb. Some develop the habit during the early months. Others never use thumbsucking at all as a way of soothing themselves.

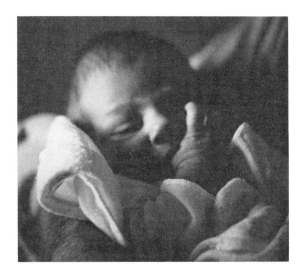

Generally, if a baby sucks his thumb during the first few months, he is not likely to give it up for four or five years. It is difficult to stop a child from thumbsucking. If you try, you're likely to be more frustrated than successful. Your child will outgrow it.

The infant should not be put to bed with a bottle, because the sugar in formula is harmful to his growing teeth. If he seems to be thirsty between feedings, he can be given slightly sweet water. (The water should be sweetened with sugar, not honey, since honey has been found to be harmful for many children under one year of age.) In the evening, the infant can suck on the breast longer, since the mother's milk is low at that time and there is little danger of the child becoming too full.

If you have a baby who cries regularly, you'll probably be quite distraught. There's no need, however, to waste your energies feeling guilty—feeling that you are somehow the cause of the baby's distress. If you know your baby isn't hungry, cold, naked, or ill and you have tried every soothing strategy you can think of, do yourself a favor and turn to experienced friends and neighbors for help. You will find some relief in discovering that others have been through the same trauma and survived. They will probably have some suggestions and may offer to relieve you during the crying hours. They know what you are going through, and your baby's crying doesn't bother other people nearly as much as it bothers you. Your baby will eventually outgrow these crying periods; believe it or not, that will take some adjustment on your part, too!

Remember also that all your babies will be different. You may have a placid first baby and a fussy, crying second baby. That's perfectly normal. If you're envious of your neighbor's happy, tearless newborn, rest assured that all children cry and whine and make life difficult sooner or later. A quiet baby may turn into an easily frustrated toddler who cries because his expectations exceed his developing capacities. Parenting, in sum, involves dealing with crying children.

Communication
So many ways!

We tend to think of communication as people talking with each other. Communication takes many forms, however; you and your infant communicate from the very first day. Here are some of the ways.

Crying. The infant very quickly develops a range of cries that signal different things. As you begin to distinguish the cries, it will become easier to know how to respond. A whimper, for example, may mean the infant is

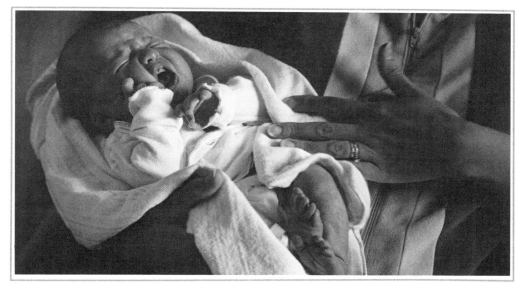

The most frustrating cry for you will be the times when the infant is crying for no apparent reason.

hungry. More energetic cries often signal distress, so a quick check to see what's the matter is a good idea.

Cooing. An infant makes a variety of sounds which are pleasing to adults. When she is cooing respond to her with coos, with speech, or with touch.

Physical movements. Some infants are expressive with their hands, arms, or legs. When they are excited or happy or content, they will move their limbs—sometimes vigorously, sometimes gently, depending on their personality and mood. As you learn to watch a baby's movements, you can become very skilled at reading what is going on inside her.

Facial expressions. Several days after birth the infant can smile. While this is a reflex action at first, soon after the first month your infant can be

When the Infant Is Awake...

During the first month of life, the infant sleeps most of the time. His waking hours are taken up by feeding, changing, bathing, and cuddling. But he will begin to spend more and more time alone and awake before calling for you.

What can you do for your baby when he is alone and awake? First, give him something to look at. Since an infant this young cannot yet distinguish a single object from a jumble of objects, it's a good idea to limit what he can see. A fancy (and expensive) mobile or crib toy is not necessarily a good idea. Instead, a brightly colored round object can be suspended above the crib; or a picture of a face, cut from a magazine, can be pasted to the side of the crib where the infant looks when he is bedded down.

Change the baby's perspective—the direction he is facing in the crib, or the location of the crib. When you put him in the crib, place him on his stomach, with his head turned in one direction or the other. This leaves him in a position to push with his arms and legs against the bed—a good muscle exercise. This is also a position many infants find consoling. Generally an infant will let you know when a position is not comfortable. It's good to vary the positions so he can get used to viewing the world from a variety of perspectives.

If there are times when the infant is awake and placed in a baby seat, make sure to position it so he has interesting things to look at. Set the seat by a window, or near children who are playing. The infant seat can be a real help at times. When you need to be free to do other things and you want the infant near you, use it. But watch out that you don't overuse it. The infant also needs time to be on the floor, on his stomach or back.

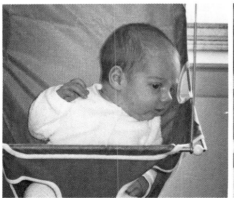

seen smiling *in response to you.* Your pleasure at receiving this first smile will support the infant's attempts to smile again and communicate with you; infants can feel the warmth intended in your smile.

"Making faces" is an especially pleasurable communication game. Infants love it when adults imitate their facial expressions. In addition, making faces helps an infant learn to recognize a face in a variety of positions and forms.

Looking. While her vision is not completely developed, the newborn is able to focus on an object eight to twelve inches away. By the end of the

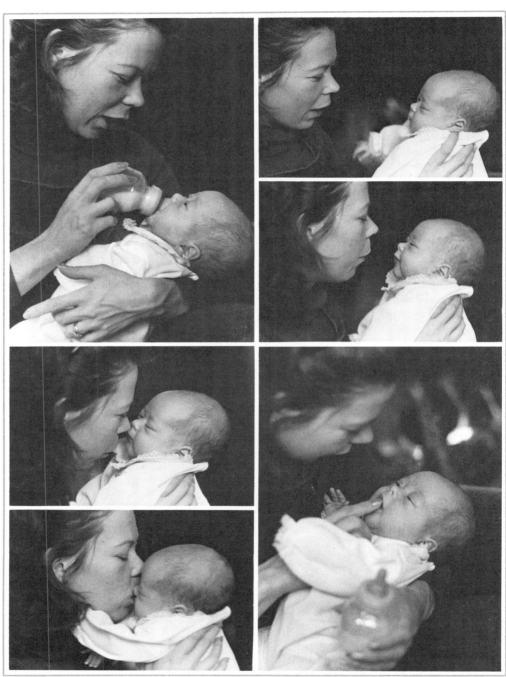

Talking to the baby is always a good activity. Sound, eye contact, and touch are the three important ways adults communicate with infants, and even if your infant doesn't understand your words, speaking to her is an expression of your love and support.

first month, she can follow with her eyes an object moved slowly from one side to another.

Looking at each other is a way of communicating that you and your infant can engage in for relatively long periods of time. It is an important kind of communication, because looking is one of the infant's best ways of beginning to understand and recognize the world around her. Very quickly the infant learns to recognize her primary caregiver. One of the signals of this recognition is the infant's gaze.

Touch. You have several ways of communicating support, love, security, and emotions (both positive and negative) to your infant. Touch is a major one. Besides the fact that the infant is learning to use her eyes and ears for communicating, her whole body is set up to receive "messages." Often an infant will be consoled by being held, touched, patted, or rubbed. At other times, touch can be the focus of a game.

Speech. Because infants do not yet understand words, many adults forget to talk to them. But infants are sensitive to speech; you should speak, coo, sing, and make sounds. The infant's awareness of sounds and rhythms shows in the movements she makes. The baby talk that many adults use instinctively is good because it slows down the normal rhythms and is pitched higher, making it easier for the infant to distinguish and respond to the sounds.

Many parents find talking to their newborns a joyful experience, a way of expressing their own delight in their own new little child. While their "talk" may be a series of repeated nonsense syllables ("a da da da da doo"), the crooning of nursery rhymes, or a singsong narrative ("We're walking along the road, we're walking along the road, Susanna and I, Susanna and I, we're walking along the road"), it nonetheless tells the baby she is important enough to talk to and that making some kind of organized noise is a primary means of expression.

The Heads Up time will pass very quickly, although during those nightly feedings it won't feel like it is passing nearly quickly enough. During this stage you will come to know many things about your infant. You will learn that she isn't as fragile as you thought. You'll be able to see the ways she has learned to respond to her new world, and you'll recognize the ways you have learned to respond to her. In the next stage, her skills and abilities will increase, and this will require new responses from you.

Things to Do

Oh Look!

The infant can only focus on objects within a very limited area—about eight to twelve inches away from her face. To give her practice in focusing, take a brightly colored object and hold it within her range. See if you can get her to focus on the object. If she doesn't, move it very slowly to see if she will follow the object. She is not likely to be able to follow it very far. When she loses sight of it, try again.

Face-to-Face

During those times when your infant is awake and not eating, spend time getting to know her. Move your face into her view. Look her in the eye, catch her gaze. Try to keep her looking at you for as long as possible. When she turns to look elsewhere, try to get her attention once again. Talk to her while you are playing with her in this way.

Hold On!

Place your finger in your infant's hand to feel the strength of her grasp. She may or may not hold on for a long time. When she lets go, put your finger in her hand once again. Gently pull against her grasp, bringing her to a sitting position momentarily. Be sure to support her with your other hand as you pull her up since she may let go at any moment.

Sensations

Don't be afraid to touch your infant even though she seems so little and fragile. Infants at this stage enjoy being touched and rubbed gently—from their heads to their toes. During this stage infants are being introduced to the world through their senses. Your touching and rubbing will help your infant begin to know what she is all about.

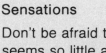

Are You Talking to Yourself?

While talking to the child will not get you a word (or even much of a sound) in response, your one-sided conversation will help introduce the child to the world of sounds. So, when you are with her, while feeding, bathing, and changing her, talk to her in soothing tones. Tell her about what you are doing. Describe what she looks like and how she is acting.

Music, Music, Music

Music can have a very calming, soothing effect on your infant. When the infant has trouble settling down, play soft music and rock her in rhythm to the music, or dance with her to the rhythm of the music. This not only calms her, but also introduces her to rhythm.

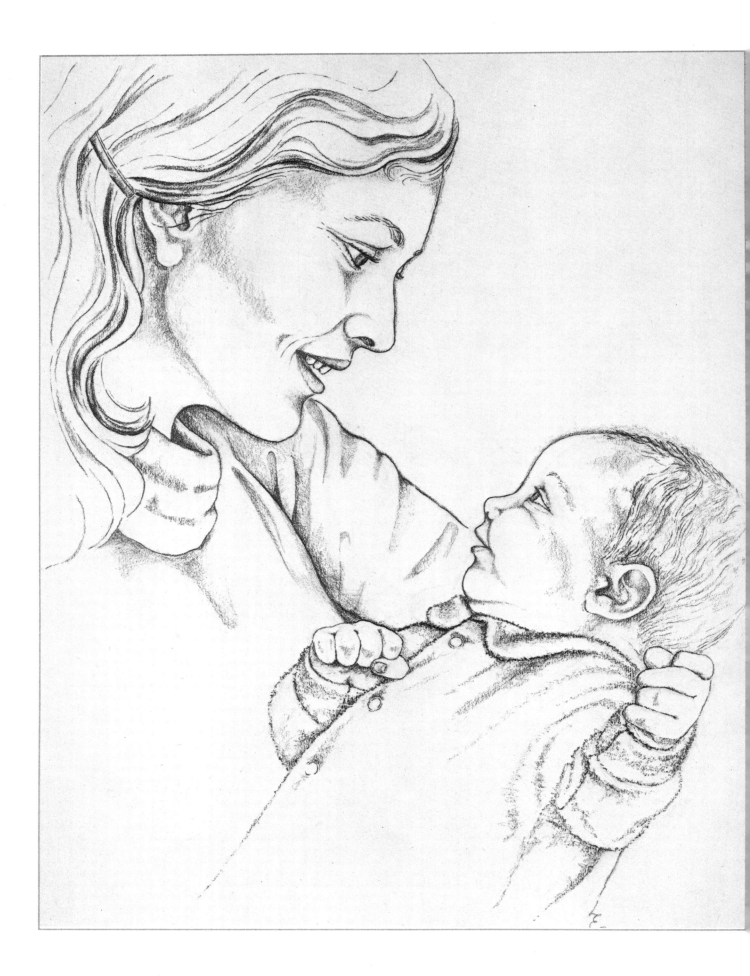

Chapter III

Your infant has gone through a period of adjustment to being in the world. By the time she enters what we call the Looker stage, she has established patterns of eating and sleeping, although these patterns may not be regular or convenient and will continue to change. Anywhere from the fourth week to  **The Looker** to the third or fourth month, she will begin to sleep through the night; this represents a significant change in her life from the adult's point of view. There are also changes in the infant's behavior which are significant from *her* point of view. A major change, as the name of this stage indicates, is that the baby increases her "looking" activity.

The infant's vision improves to a near-adult sharpness. Her range of vision expands from what is in front of her nose to what is above and to the sides of her. She appears, at times, to be soaking in the world through her eyes. This is a very important experience for her later learning: the more she looks, the better she gets at seeing things. She develops some control of her looking, choosing which objects to focus on and which to turn away from. When she can control her looking, she has a way to communicate with you.

This visual development goes along with a general trend in the infant's growth. She is awake for longer hours, so there are awake times when she

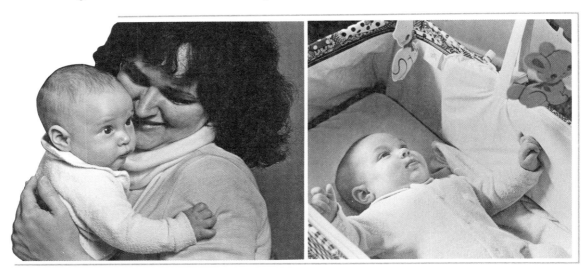

The Looker stage is a time when there is a widening in the infant's perceptions. Looking at faces and objects and listening to voices and sounds are good activities for her. Many babies will stare intently at a lamp or overhead light when placed near it. Others love gazing at a brightly colored object.

is not being fed, changed, or bathed; sights and sounds occupy her attention during these times. Since she's been around for several weeks already, events have occurred with enough regularity that they are now familiar and expected. She responds more to voices and appears more alert.

The infant is faced with so many different situations and stimuli, it is a wonder how quickly and well she is able to sort them out. Her instincts, perceptions, emotions, nerves, and muscles are all developing simultaneously; to support your infant's development means to support all of these.

Because the infant's abilities and awareness develop gradually, she will need protection against overstimulation. Infants can do this for themselves to some extent. Many can fall asleep in the middle of a loud, crowded room; it's as if there is an automatic switch-off which protects them from being overwhelmed. But your infant needs your help. Supporting your infant's development means helping her get the right amount of stimulation—neither too much nor too little. This takes careful observation and thought on your part. A crib that's loaded down with mobiles and pictures and lace trim and decals is too much for the infant to take in with her unpracticed eyes. On the other hand, bare crib walls and a bare ceiling do not offer the infant much practice in looking.

People generally expect the infant to level off emotionally during this period, to resemble more closely the advertiser's image of a gurgling, contented baby. This, of course, depends very much on her temperament and her adjustment to her family and home. But there is a general increase of interest in what is going on around her. An infant quickly learns to look at objects which give her pleasure and to seek pleasure with her eyes and ears.

The infant develops physically in a number of ways. She learns to sustain a sitting position. She learns to hold her head steady, to turn it at will in order to follow moving objects with her eyes, to lift it when she is lying on her stomach and can't see. (She may learn to lift her entire upper torso in a kind of mini-pushup, in order to look at something that interests her.) Her body movements become stronger and smoother, and within a few months she is able to move both sides of her body in unison. All of this physical and perceptual work gives the infant a footing for more active exploration of the world.

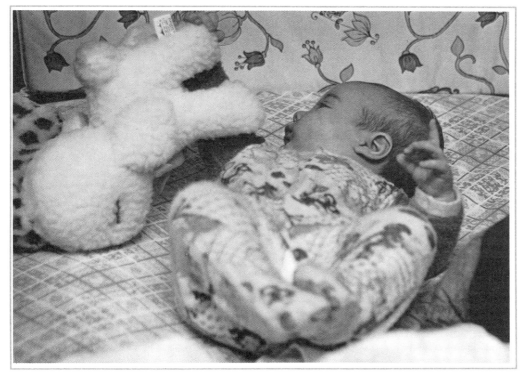

The Looker stage is also a time when muscles are developing and the infant is gaining greater control.

Organizing Your Days

Your infant is much more alert and awake now for longer periods of time, so he will be able to spend more time exploring. However, he can also get bored, so there have to be a variety of experiences available to him to challenge his exploratory interest. In order to provide these experiences, you will need to become an organizer in your own home. If you spend time reacting, reacting, and reacting again to demands, your baby (and perhaps other family members) will run you ragged. So learn to think ahead. What is the baby's schedule? What will you need to do with him and for him as the day progresses? What do you expect from the other family members? Are you able to make times for yourself to relax and do something enjoyable, both alone and with your child?

How is the work shared in your family? Mothers often take practically all the responsibility for the infant's care. Fathers and other family members often expect this of the mother. It may or may not be desirable for a mother to play this role. It depends on her needs and interests and family circumstances. It is important to sit down regularly with your family and with caregivers to discuss what the baby needs, who will provide for these needs, how and when they'll be provided for. It's also a good idea to discuss events in the baby's day. Some families like to jot down what they notice about their infant—the activities the infant enjoys, the situations that are not smooth and comfortable, the feelings they have about parenting; this is especially helpful in households where one or both parents are usually away from home during the day. The companion volume to this book, *Good Beginnings: A Baby's Diary,* can guide such observations.

Often, new fathers who felt nervous about the baby in his first few months begin to relax and want to be more involved in the baby's care. Talking together about the infant is a good way for everyone to get into the habit of paying attention to the infant's growth. It also makes it less likely that working parents will miss out on this critical time in their child's development.

Having a regular routine will help you stay on top of things. A routine is more than knowing the time the baby will eat, nap, have a bath, and go to bed. It is also *how* these things are done. This is not to suggest that you set up rigid rules, but it may help at mealtime, for example, if you take a minute each morning to plan the day's menu. Stop to make sure you have all the ingredients you need. Have a routine for feeding the infant. This gives him something to count on, and you won't have to work as hard each time to let him know what you expect. It also gives you a chance to relax—*you* know what to expect, too.

Sense of Self
Temperament

One change that is likely to occur in the infant's life after the first month is that you and the infant will be seeing more and more people. Relatives and friends will be dropping by to see the baby now that your routine is getting back to normal. Each new person will have comments to make. "She's a beautiful baby." "She's too calm." "He looks uneasy." "That one is a tiger." You, too, can get caught up in this game. Who is this new person? "He's a real charmer." "She's so active we can barely keep up with her." "He is the quiet, thoughtful type." These comments can provide you with useful insights, but you need to be aware of the pitfall of "labeling" the child.

Labeling is not necessarily bad and can be descriptive of the child's temperament. Telling yourself you have a "fussy" baby may make it easier for you to tolerate her crying. On the other hand, adults sometimes label a child and then get into the habit of responding in set ways. For example, a naturally quiet baby may be left to her own devices too often because caregivers see her as "self-sufficient." A "fussy" baby may be deliberately ignored in her squalling and have no way to calm herself. Remember, too, that even at their best, labels only describe certain aspects of any infant. Your baby may be "fussy" in the afternoon when visitors come, but happy and playful during the morning hours when the house is relatively quiet. Also, infants change and outgrow their labels at an amazing rate.

Each infant has her own temperament, but what does that mean? We have identified the following six aspects of temperament to help you in watching your infant for special characteristics. While these are not the only elements that make up temperament, by considering them in combination you can get an idea of just what distinguishes your infant from all other infants.

Activity level. This refers to how much your infant moves. Many infants are all over the place right from the start. You come in when the infant wakes to find that she has turned herself completely around in the crib; and she simply never keeps a blanket on for more than ten minutes. Or your infant may be less active—you always find her in exactly the same place you left her, and all the covers are neatly tucked in.

How much does your baby move around, and how often? Is she still for long periods of time? If so, when do they occur? Do active periods always follow certain events, such as feeding time, or do they vary? In what ways is your child active? With her whole body? With her face or voice only?

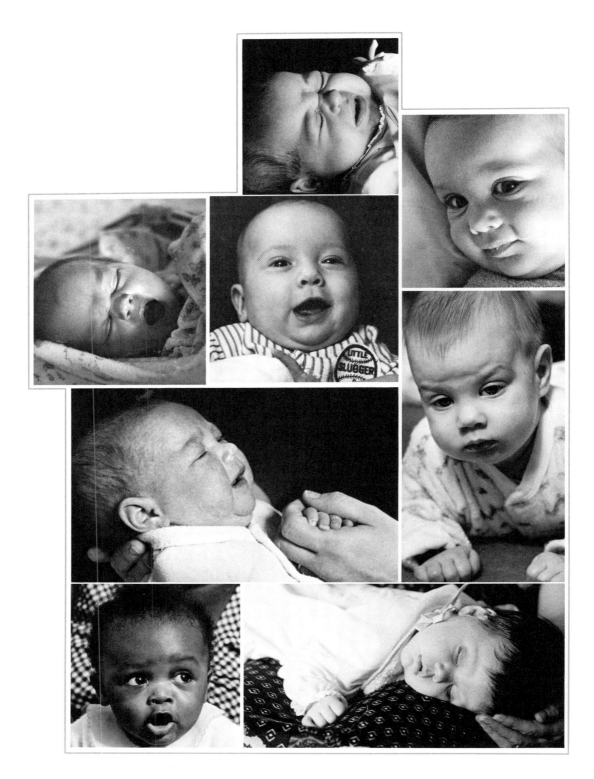

When you are dressing or feeding her, how much squirming or twisting and turning does she do? When she is lying alone on the floor or bassinette, how much does she move? Does she often kick the covers off or change her position (from stomach to back, from foot of bed to head)? Is she more active when she is aware of people in the room with her, or when she can't see them?

Adaptability to change. This refers to the ease with which your infant is able to adapt to new situations. Some infants can be moved from one bed to another and fall asleep with ease in all situations. Other infants are very sensitive to changes in the bedroom. If the crib is turned in a different direction, they will know it. If they are taken to someone else's house for the afternoon or evening, they will be unable to fall asleep in the "strange" environment.

How predictable is your baby in her eating, sleeping, and bowel movements? Can you usually predict when she'll want to eat and how hungry she'll be? If circumstances demand a change in routine (a trip to the doctor, a family picnic), how does it affect her? Does it affect her eating habits, her sleep, her mood, her responsiveness to the people around her? If your infant is quite unscheduled and erratic, can you identify any patterns at all? Are the longer periods between feedings linked to any events in the household? Are the shorter ones? What happened in your home a day or two before a time that was especially difficult for your baby? (Visitors? Job change? Holiday festivities?) Do you find yourself adapting to the baby's schedule, or can you expect her to adjust to a schedule that is convenient for both of you?

Attention. Attention refers to the amount of time the infant sticks with one thing. Some infants will spend a long time looking at an object; others can be shown an object, take it in with a quick glance, and be ready for something else.

What kind of attention span does your baby have, and how does it vary for different types of activities (looking, moving, making sounds, feeding)? How long will your baby stick with something if it's especially difficult? How does your baby deal with interruptions? Is she easily distracted, or does she appear to have her own idea about what to focus on? How much does she resist experiences she doesn't like, such as bathtime or eating a new food?

Preferences. Some people like sports, others like classical music; some are fascinated by antique cars, others spend hours developing science fiction futures. Infants also show preferences. What catches your baby's interest? Does she respond especially to sounds, to certain people, to what she sees outside the window? When she is in her infant seat, what does she focus on? Which aspects of her seem to be developing more rapidly than others—her physical movements, her sound-making, her looking or listening, her responses to and delight in people? Does your infant prefer one object (to gaze at) over others? What games does she like?

Responses. A wink, a raised eyebrow, a wave of the hand may be the response that one adult would give in a situation which would bring an embrace, a gasp, a faint from another adult. How much we respond physically and emotionally to an event varies greatly from adult to adult. The same thing happens with infants. Some are very easily startled and take a long time to be soothed; others are relatively unaffected by sudden noises and calm themselves when distressed.

How does your baby respond to events, pleasant and unpleasant? How intensely does she respond? For example, if she is upset, does she scream and wail, or does she merely frown or squirm? How do her responses vary from one situation to another? Are there certain kinds of experiences which make her respond more actively? Does she seem to have a lot of energy to put into eating, fussing, moving around in her seat? Does she startle frequently or easily at loud noises? How do bright lights affect

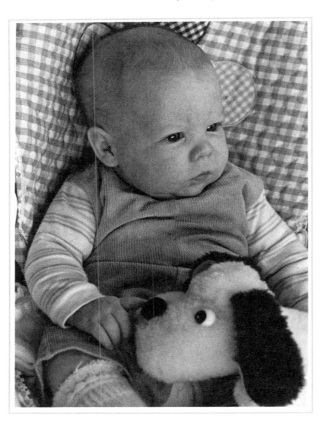

her? Does she seem ruffled by activity around her? Does she withdraw when overwhelmed? Is she bothered by scratchy clothes or changes in temperature? Does she take mild pain in stride, or react with a howl?

Mood. How would you describe your baby's overall mood—generally quiet, generally exuberant? What causes her mood to shift? How does her mood differ at different times of day? How sensitive is she to the moods of people around her? If you are in a bad mood, does she pick up on it, shift moods herself? To what extent is her mood affected by the attention of others? How do transition times (going to sleep at night, waking up from a nap, eating after playing) affect her mood? How much help does she need to control her moods? How does she communicate her moods to you?

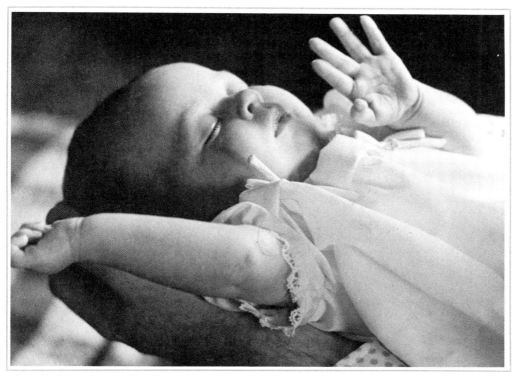

As you learn to predict how your infant will react to various situations, you can begin to relax. You will feel more comfortable about being able to meet her demands.

These questions about your baby's temperament will be answered over time in a variety of situations. Many of these situations will recur daily as you are caring for her. The things you do with your infant during feeding, bathing, diapering, and those longer awake times will help you learn more about the kind of person she is.

Physical Abilities
Refinements and discoveries

The infant's physical growth during these months is especially exciting and satisfying to parents and caregivers. She grows from a tiny bundle to a small robust person. She is less fragile and more active and responsive. She no longer needs to be supported at the neck, which means she has more control of her "looking." The trend in physical development, as far as control goes, is from top to bottom: the infant learns to use her eyes and ears and learns to bring her hand to her mouth and learns what her face feels like long before she realizes that she has toes. Her torso becomes stronger and is able to support her weight (in a sitting position) before her legs do (for crawling).

Central to this stage, of course, is all the looking the infant does. She will regard a face for long periods of time, especially a familiar face. Studies done with infants have shown that they enjoy the exaggerated faces people make at them. However, if the grimaces become too extreme, the baby will cease to watch, or will become upset. It is important for you and your infant to spend time gazing at each other. You are doing more than teaching her the parts of a human face when you are with her in this way—you are sharing yourself with her.

The infant's vision is improving in two ways. First, her eyesight is becoming stronger, so she can focus

The infant spends a lot of her time gazing. She appears to be memorizing the shape and parts of the human face.

on objects which are further away. Second, her ability to focus on objects and distinct shapes is improving. (Her neck helps her in this—it's stronger, and she is learning to turn it at will.) Early on in this stage she is able to look at objects on both sides of her and above her. This means that she can turn to look at something, and that she can stop looking and turn away from something if she wishes.

Along with seeing, the infant's hearing becomes more refined; now she will turn to locate sounds in the room, coordinating her vision and hearing. She will seek out familiar sounds. For example, if you enter the room talking, the infant may turn her head to see you. You can give your infant many experiences with sounds, such as calling to her from across the room, or holding a music box in different places so she will turn to look at it. These experiences give her practice in linking sights and sounds, and in anticipating a familiar sight when she hears a familiar sound. (She is also beginning to anticipate events. When either the bottle or breast appears, she may make sucking motions with her mouth.)

Besides linking what is around her by seeing and hearing, your infant is also gradually learning about her own body, and strengthening it.

The smile, which first appears as a reflex, soon comes under the baby's control; it is something she can use to express pleasure. Many babies seem to smile with their whole bodies, waving their arms and legs, cooing, gurgling, bouncing. Their capacity for pleasure is growing during this time, and they enjoy games which include other people—smiling, making

sounds, having air blown softly on their stomachs. Your baby will quickly learn to be a participant in such games, egging you on with encouraging sounds and movements and squealing with pleasure. Be sure to look for signs that she is tiring of the game, or is becoming overstimulated—she may look away, begin to cry, or suddenly quiet down.

Your baby's neck is steady now and needs less support. This added strength allows her to turn her head—in fact her neck becomes even

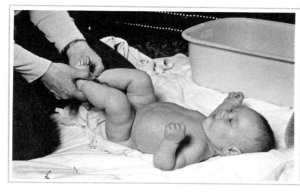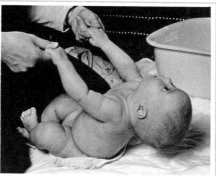

Help your baby learn to coordinate her body by making "games" out of exercise activities.

stronger through her attempts to turn and lift her head. She can now lift herself by bringing her chin up when she is lying on her stomach. Also while on her stomach, your baby may begin to move her knees up and scramble with her arms; this is not a controlled attempt to crawl, but it is good practice. When lying on her back, she will often "bicycle," first in a kind of jerky, flailing motion, and then later with smoother, larger arcs. You can make this into a game, holding the infant's feet and bicycling gently with her. After some practice, the movements become more coordinated and balanced. More active babies can do this frequently; other, quieter ones might do it hardly at all. But whether the infant is actively practicing or quiet and relatively inactive, she *will* learn to coordinate her body.

The infant eventually discovers her hand, as it wanders in and out of her field of vision. She soon learns to bring it to the midline (the center of her body) so she can gaze at it, examine it, and bring it to her mouth—another kind of exploration. Although infants in the womb can suck their fists, they gain control of this action during this particular stage. Bringing her fist to her mouth and sucking is one way an infant can console herself; at the same time she is establishing a link between two vital exploratory tools— the hand and the mouth. Later, the child will use her hands to reach toward and grasp objects.

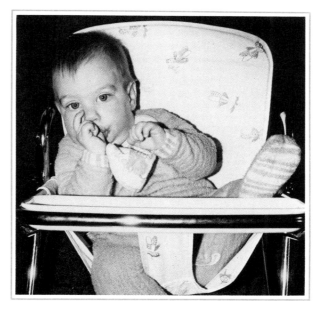

When the baby discovers her hand and learns to bring it to her mouth, she has found a way to console and calm herself.

In the Looker stage, the infant begins to recognize things and becomes increasingly curious and responsive to the sensations presented by the world around her.

Understanding the World
Seeing with her own eyes

Throughout her first year of life, your infant's understanding of the world around her, her cognitive development, is closely linked to her physical development. As her ability to look is expanding, so too is her ability to respond to what she sees.

It takes many experiences with an object for the infant to become familiar with it, and even longer for her to "know" it, in the sense of forming a concept of it. At first only bright, distinct objects in her line of vision would hold her attention. Now she gazes for a longer time and at a wider range of objects. She also learns to handle a wider range of sounds and isn't as easily startled. She is becoming familiar with her surroundings and is beginning to scrutinize them. A moving lamp that throws shifting patterns on the wall will give her something to look at and follow, whereas earlier it would have been distracting. Pictures on the sides of the crib (or on the ceiling) and dangling crib toys are "educational" for her now. She likes being near a window so she can look outside. A mirror will invariably catch her attention. Bring your infant into the room where you are working and set her up so she can see what is going on. Look around to make sure there are plenty of things to interest her. If you have an infant who is cooing and gurgling and responding to sounds around her, or even if your infant is fairly quiet, you will want to make sure that there are many interesting sounds for her to listen to.

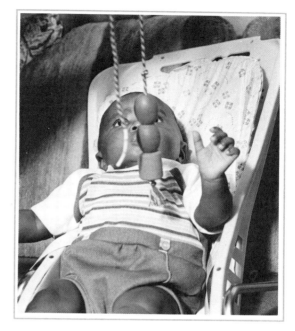

Interesting things happen "accidentally" to the infant at this stage. While she is delighted when a rattle makes a noise after she swings her arm, she is not aware that *she* is shaking the rattle and making the noise. In her mind, the two events are linked, but she doesn't understand her role in the process. Similarly, when she kicks her feet, the mobile may begin to swing; she sees that the mobile is swinging and is delighted, but she doesn't realize that *her* feet are kicking the string and causing the mobile to move.

The infant wants you to respond to her and to repeat your actions. She is pleased when you smile and talk to her in response to her cooing. She will want you to "do it again" when you make a face that causes her to laugh. When you imitate her gestures she will begin to understand more about the connection between her actions and people's responses to her.

Infants at this stage form preferences for objects, people, and activities and will consistently choose "favorites." Having preferences means making choices, and making choices demonstrates mental skills; it requires recognition, recollection, and judgment.

Yet objects are events as far as the infant is concerned: their existence is fleeting. Your baby can now follow objects with her eyes as you move them in front of her. She will watch them until they disappear, but she will keep her eyes focused on the spot where they disappeared for only a short time. She is unconcerned that the object is gone. As long as it is in sight, she will be interested in it. But when it is out of sight, it is out of mind, even though she will show obvious delight in seeing the familiar object again. She will grasp a toy that is placed in her hand, but when the toy falls, she won't look for it, nor will she be aware of where it has gone. So during this stage, while you can expect the infant to have a favorite toy, she will not be upset when her toys are not with her. The need for the favorite toy to accompany her everywhere will come later.

In sum, the objects that the Looker has in view are of great interest to her, and she wants to explore them; but she does not understand that they still exist when she doesn't see them—nor does she care.

Relationships
A growing awareness of others

One mom and infant looked forward to getting the mail together every day. On the way down the driveway, the infant squirmed with delight as she watched the family dog frisking along beside them. Next they played repeated games of "open and shut the mailbox" followed by "peek-a-boo" with various pieces of mail as they walked back up the driveway.

Evenings were Dick's favorite time with his infant daughter. Lying on her back on his knees she'd coo and wiggle while her daddy gently rolled a soft, cylindrical sofa pillow from her head all the way down to her toes.

Your infant needs to be cuddled. She needs to be spoken to and responded to when she "speaks." She needs to be included in the life of the household. Early on she learned to recognize you and to respond to your voice. Now she is learning to recognize siblings and other household members, and may have very different responses to each, depending on the type of interactions she has had with them.

The infant can match her movements to the rhythm of those she knows. If one were to portray the rhythm of an infant and mother doing something together, or just *being* together, it might be said to resemble a softly undulating wave; the rhythm of the infant and father would be different, perhaps a wave with higher and sharper peaks and deeper troughs. The

Your infant is learning to develop different relationships with different people. She uses all of her senses and her experiences to do this. She also comes up with her own ways of responding to different individuals.

infant's relationship with a stranger probably wouldn't have a discernible shape, since their rhythms would never quite match and might in fact be at cross-purposes.

The infant is also more aware now of an adult's feelings. She is able to sense the moods of adults she knows well—she knows when they are sad, depressed, content, animated. She is also able to recognize familiar adults by their smell. There appears to be some truth in the advice passed down from grandmother to granddaughter over the years: "Don't change your perfume when you have an infant around." She sets great store by the familiarity of your appearance; a new hairstyle, for example, can be very upsetting to a child in the first year.

Since the infant isn't the only person in the household with needs, make sure you recognize what your needs are too, and think about how and when you can spend time with your infant. Often, when time is limited, you become so anxious that even during the time you have for your infant you feel rushed and tense. Neither of you can relax and enjoy being together. When you are with your baby, try to focus your attention on her; put aside all other things in your life for a while. This will help make the time you spend together secure, supportive, and interesting for the infant. These don't have to be lengthy "sessions." They can be the five or ten minutes you talk with your child, provide her with an interesting toy, look for her response to your voice. These times together can be a regular part of your daily routine.

It will take time to learn to recognize when to continue play with the infant and when to stop. Sometimes when games are carried on too long, the infant becomes overstimulated; she gets "hyper." She is wound up and has a hard time settling down. Frequently, adults get a child into this state by carrying a game to a fever pitch. The child seems to enjoy the game, but it may have gone beyond the point where she can let you know it should be stopped. If this happens, it's important for you to step out of the game and calm your infant.

It may take you a while to recognize when the baby is overstimulated. After a few games that end with the baby upset, however, you will begin to pick up cues earlier. In these instances you can provide a calm activity as a transition from the rowdy game to restful sleep. It may be helpful to hold the infant, to gently restrain flailing arms and legs, to gently rub her tummy or back. Sometimes you simply need to leave her alone so that she can calm herself.

Communication
Sounds and gestures

Infants in this stage begin to communicate by exchanging looks and glances and by gesturing. Communication also occurs through touching and holding. As you become aware of what your infant is doing, you will notice the variety of ways she expresses what she wants, needs, and feels. From the first hours infants cry, and the older they get, the more differentiated their cries become. You'll be able to recognize when the infant

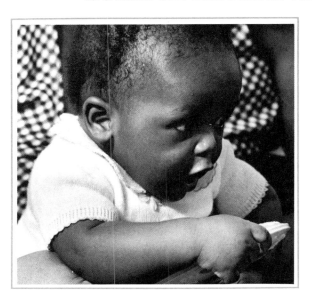

is hungry, tired, uncomfortable, or bored. The seemingly "uncaused" crying of the first month or two is likely to decrease. The infant now has other ways of communicating with you.

When your baby makes sounds, you can imitate them and it becomes a game. Sometimes the sounds she makes are a kind of "conversation" with you. It can be an enjoyable activity to talk to the baby in response to her coos and gurgles. The baby will come to know when your attention is focused on a conversation with someone else. She'll try to join in adult conversations by contributing her own sounds.

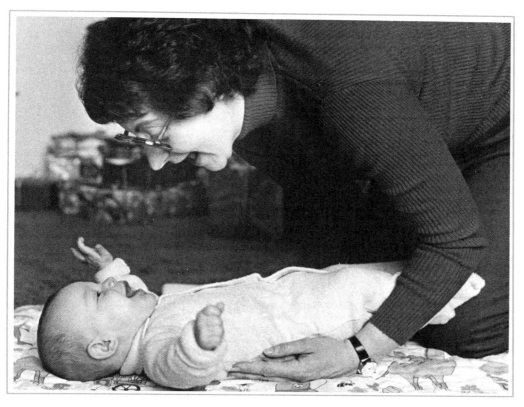

The infant is exploring her ability to make sounds and gradually expanding her repertoire of sounds. It's both fun and helpful for you to pay attention to the sounds the infant is making and to repeat them back to her.

Another "language" which the infant comes to use more and more is that of facial expressions and physical gestures. She learns to smile at people she knows, to frown when confused or unhappy, to bounce around or wave her arms with delight.

During the Looker stage your infant has changed in many ways. Her personality is now more evident, she is able to give you better cues about what she wants and needs, and you can begin to see the ways in which she is developing an interest in people and things. All of these events have occurred while she's been relatively immobile—*you* have had control of where she goes and when. In the next stage, a new dimension will be added as the infant begins to get around on her own.

Things to Do

Looking for a Response

Hum or sing softly to your child, then stop and watch to see if she gives some sign of having heard you—she may become very still, make sounds herself, wave her arms and legs, watch you intently. Repeat the sound again and see if she acts in the same way this time when you stop. If you cannot see any response, you may not have her attention. Try again, or wait until another time.

Choosing a Play Time

Try playing with the infant at different times during the day—after feeding, in the morning, in the evening, before she goes to sleep, when you are the most relaxed, when she seems to be the most alert. What time works best for both of you? The timing won't always be perfect. There will be days when no time is a good time. In those instances try again the next day!

Starting a Conversation With the Looker

Make a sound that the infant frequently makes, in order to get her to imitate the sound. This can be done in a variety of situations (while she's being held or diapered, when she's looking in a mirror, when she's holding a toy). To vary this activity, use a relatively new sound that the infant has made only a few times.

Reaching Out

Offer the infant a toy she can grasp. Put it near her hand within her sight. If she wants it, she will reach for it and try to grasp it. Make sure it is within her range so that she can reach and hold it. Materials you might use are: rattles with thin handles, clothespins, small plastic spoons, squeaker toys, soft stuffed animals with legs or arms the infant can grasp. For variations on this activity, change the infant's position. Play with her when she is sitting or when she is lying on her back. You can also change the location of the object. You can put it anywhere between the infant's waist and eye level, on either side. Show her two objects at the same time. Now she has a choice. Which one does she go after? the new toy? the familiar toy? the one that is always on the right or left? Does it matter what color the object is?

Getting to Know You

Observe how your infant is getting to know you and others in the household. One thing to look for is how long she continues to watch someone. She will want to keep looking at persons she knows. But she may turn away more rapidly or be reluctant to give her attention to strangers. How do you get her to watch you and maintain eye contact with you even when she begins to turn away? Talk to her while you are communicating through your eyes. She'll appreciate your undivided attention.

Strengthening the Looker's Vision

Hold two different-colored objects so that the infant can easily see them. First move one slowly until the infant is looking at it, then move the other slowly, alternating the movement to get the infant to look from one object to the other. You can also use noisemaking objects, such as rattles.

Chapter IV

The name *Creeper-Crawler* suggests a major turning point for your infant—the emergence of the ability to make and carry out some choices about where she is going to be and what she is going to do.

The Creeper-Crawler

As she begins to creep and crawl, your infant begins to be more independent; at the same time she demands attention and the assurance that you are there to back her up. She becomes increasingly alert and interested in things and wants to be included more in what is going on around her. She learns to grasp objects she sees and to bring them to her mouth. She is no longer a spectator, so you'll need to begin thinking about "babyproofing" your house; that attractive but fragile mobile you hung up for your Looker will have to be replaced with something more durable. Breakable things, such as vases, will soon need to be moved to higher places so they don't get knocked over once your baby starts to crawl. But extra caution should be balanced by extra attention to the job of providing a stimulating environment for your more active baby.

In many ways this is a stage of contrasts. While the infant is able to attempt more things, she is also frustrated by her limitations. At the beginning of the Creeper-Crawler period, your infant can *almost* do a number of things—almost sit alone, almost crawl about, almost do what she appears to want to do with objects. As she progresses through this stage, she will become more accomplished. But because of her "almost" abilities, there are frustrations at every turn! Her idea of what she wants to do almost always precedes her ability to do it.

Physical Abilities
From discoveries to games to skills

In the first couple of months of the Creeper-Crawler stage, your infant will still be immobile and uncoordinated. But there are several important developments which will set the stage for her first attempts to crawl and to sit upright.

One of the earliest of these developments is the infant's discovery of her feet and toes. She has found the lower boundaries of her body. Since

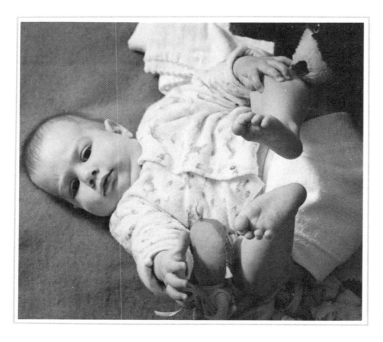

mobility requires coordination and use of the top and bottom of her body, this discovery is a signal that she is entering the Creeper-Crawler stage. Now, instead of merely reacting to her various body parts as she happens upon them, she begins to get a sense of herself as a whole person, separate from her surroundings.

Another important development is learning to roll herself over, from her stomach to her back, much to her surprise. (She won't be able to roll from back to stomach until

the next stage.) She may not like being on her back, and you'll find your-self repeatedly responding to her cries of distress when she can't reverse her action. She will recognize that she has done something really new—you'll be able to tell from the look on her face—and will repeat her action to see if she can do it again. For most babies, accidental discoveries quickly turn into games and eventually into skills.

In her attempts to crawl, the baby will often find herself facing a new view or pointed in a new direction. This too is quite a discovery, and it gives her all the more reason to move herself around. The more she moves the more she sees. Eventually her movements will propel her across the floor. She begins to crawl; her movements are quite uncoordinated, but somehow they do the job. Often, at first, her efforts to go forward don't quite work and instead send her backward. But soon she has things under control and gets where she wants to go faster and faster. When the crawling begins, be sure that the child's path is safe and free of potentially dangerous obstacles.

Sitting up often happens by accident as the infant is learning to crawl: she goes backward rather than forward and gets ahead of herself; her legs get tangled up in clothing; she leans to one side to avoid the couch; or

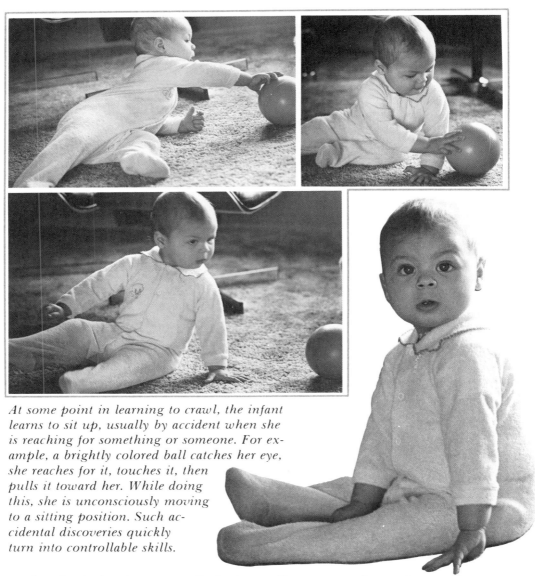

At some point in learning to crawl, the infant learns to sit up, usually by accident when she is reaching for something or someone. For example, a brightly colored ball catches her eye, she reaches for it, touches it, then pulls it toward her. While doing this, she is unconsciously moving to a sitting position. Such accidental discoveries quickly turn into controllable skills.

maybe she just gets very excited when rolling over and somehow ends up sitting. You can see on her face the mix of reactions: surprise, fear, pleasure, awe—she knows she's discovered a new trick. Often she will tumble herself back over to try again. She'll practice the skill regularly for several days, until she is sitting up like a pro.

Toward the end of this stage, many infants will be making attempts to pull themselves to an upright position. With some, it may happen that in pulling on the rungs of a chair, they find themselves on their knees. This can be scary enough, and they won't try it again for a while. Other infants might pull on the edge of a couch and suddenly find themselves unsteadily but triumphantly on their feet. It's hard to tell whether they planned it, but there they are. Getting down may be another matter, and often you will be called to the rescue.

The infant has been *reaching* for objects and people since the Looker stage. Now she is getting better and better at coordinating her eyes and hands; she can reach with greater purpose and *grasp* objects. Once she gets hold of an object, she shakes it, bangs it, tastes it; something new is in

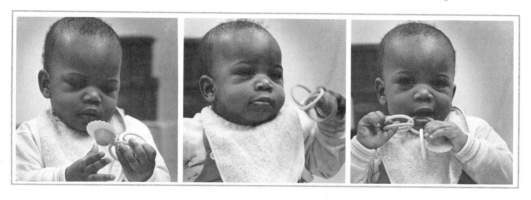

her hand, and she wants to explore it. It's easier for her to grasp slender objects than round ones. A stuffed toy that has graspable arms and legs will provide more enjoyment than a round stuffed bear that's hard to get hold of.

Your baby goes from being a watcher to being a more active participant. She now *seeks* activity as well as responds to it, so you should think about what you want to have available for her to explore during this stage. This is an excellent time to introduce rattles. The noise intrigues the infant, though she still isn't aware that it's her own action making the noise. Many infants take particular delight in crumpling paper. If you want to save your magazines, get them out of your infant's reach! Wax paper from the kitchen is perfect: it doesn't matter if it gets wrinkled, there's no ink to come off on the infant's hands or mouth, and the sound and feel of it are especially pleasing.

If you've been using a mobile with small parts, this must now be replaced with much sturdier objects. Anything within reach will be grasped, banged, tasted, and dropped. And those things you think are out of reach probably aren't unless they're more than three feet off the ground.

Equipment for Your Infant

As your infant becomes more active physically, it is important to think about the equipment you want to have, both to help him develop and as a convenience for you. Most infant equipment is designed to keep the child within a contained space—car seat, infant carrier, stroller, jump seat, playpen, walker, highchair, feeding table, back-carrier. These items can be useful. A car seat is a must, and should be used *every* time you are in the car. Other items, however, need to be used with thought.

For example, people have very strong feelings about playpens. There are parents who claim they would never use a playpen because their child hates to be cooped up. While this may be true, it may also have something to do with where the playpen is located in the house and the length of time the baby is left in it. If it is tucked away in a corner somewhere, he will become bored. If it is in a more open space where he has a variety of things to see, he is likely to be far more content. Some people keep their child in the playpen all the time because it saves them the trouble of worrying about where he is. The quiet infant may not protest, but this is generally not a good idea because it limits the infant's experience; he needs a variety of textures, sounds, and views.

Your baby has an opportunity to practice creeping and crawling in the playpen—it's a safe environment for his new mobility. The playpen can also be satisfying if there are things in and around it that attract the baby's attention and provide the stimulation he needs to learn more about his world. But he should not be confined to the playpen all the time.

On the other hand, a playpen used for short periods during specific parts of the day can be a blessing. One mother, for example, fed her Creeper-Crawler before the rest of the family and then put the infant in a playpen during the family's meal. Since the playpen was close to the table, the infant was able to take part in the family meal. And since he was nearby, no one had to leave the table to find out what he was up to.

Another mother used a playpen to protect her Creeper-Crawler from his sometimes over-exuberant sister. Two-year-old Caroline loved to play with her little brother Eddie, but after a while, Caroline's taps on Eddie's head turned to hits, and both children needed the separation the playpen provided. Sometimes, too, when Eddie crept into Caroline's block towers, Caroline got into the playpen with her blocks so she could build without interruption.

A very tempting piece of equipment to get for infants at this stage is a jumping seat that can be placed in a doorway.

The infant can be propped up in the seat and sit quite contentedly with an occasional swing from a passing adult; he can manipulate the swing enough to face either room, perhaps watching one adult in the kitchen while also keeping an eye on someone else in the living room. The jumping seat, however, if used too much, will not allow the child to develop his crawling ability. He needs a chance to be on the floor trying to push himself around. Used at certain times during the day, though, it can give a mom or dad just enough time to get a meal on the table, write a letter, or read the paper.

In deciding which equipment to have or accept as hand-me-downs, think about what the equipment allows your infant to do and learn, and how he might be limited by it. Clearly, you are the one to choose which items to use, based on your family's needs.

Relationships
Recognition of the other

During this stage the infant becomes more and more sociable. She is able to initiate games with you and let you know when she wants to continue a game. When you imitate her, she will respond by repeating the action. Although she's not consciously aware of this give-and-take, the infant is clearly beginning to understand social interaction. One of the ways she lets you know she likes your company is by showing absolute delight in what you are doing together.

She is becoming aware of who she knows and who she doesn't know. During the Heads Up and Looker stages, she was generally comfortable with a variety of people. But in this stage, as she learns to tell familiars from strangers, she may be reluctant to go to strangers, especially if a parent isn't in the room.

At this stage the infant is not at all happy to see you walk out of the room. She fears that you won't come back. This doesn't mean that you can never leave her alone; it simply means that you need to be aware of why she is clinging to you. When you leave, don't sneak away; that only reinforces the idea that you have disappeared. Let her know you are going and that you intend to return. Of course she won't really understand your words, but if your gestures and tone of voice assure her that you'll return, it will help her to develop a sense of trust. Part of what is happening at this stage is that the infant is realizing she is a separate person. She is not an extension of you, nor are you an extension of her. You are two separate people, and that can be frightening to her.

Seeing you now as a separate person, your infant will examine you more carefully. She will explore your face by touching, poking, pulling hair and ears. Dangling earrings are a prime target for grasping hands. She'll be interested in exploring the inside of your mouth and understanding how your face is put together.

Bathtimes are some of the best times to play (and talk) together. Most infants enjoy playing a few minutes with no clothes on—feeling their own body, feeling the texture of the towel. Boys at this stage generally discover their penis, and will want to explore it. If you allow a boy to explore his

Most Creeper-Crawlers won't be willing to respond positively to just anyone. Creeper-Crawlers are comfortable with people they know but uncomfortable with those they don't.

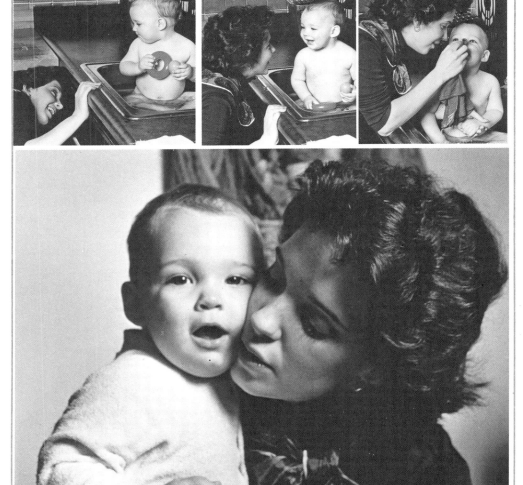

penis in the same way he explores other parts of his body, you will go a long way toward helping him be comfortable with his sexuality.

There will be more water play as the infant learns to sit up during bathtime. She will particularly enjoy splashing, and adults can join in the action. A nylon-mesh toy can create many interesting splashes. Sponges of different sizes, shapes, and colors are also good to have around during bathtime. Wrapping the infant in a warm towel at the end of the bath will make her feel loved and secure.

Infants at this stage particularly enjoy being swung gently. They love for you to bounce them on your knee or dangle them over your knees head first while you hold them by the ankles. They love having their arms stretched out and legs rotated in a bicycle movement. They delight in feeling their muscles stretched and being upside down and swinging in the air. Move with your baby to the rhythm of music. Roughhouse with her. But be careful: when children are handled too roughly they begin to fear physical contact. Playtime can be great fun for both of you, but keep it gentle and learn to recognize when it is time to stop.

The infant who has built a trusting relationship with adults, and who knows that her needs will be responded to, will open her arms and reach out to be picked up. She has learned that this signal will result in being held or moved to a different position. She won't give this signal to just any adult; she'll use it only with those she knows well and trusts.

Sense of Self
Recognition of "me"

Your infant is now aware of her whole body. She has discovered her toes and understands that they are a continuation of her trunk and legs. She is able to recognize herself in a mirror and takes great pleasure in watching herself. Here are the beginnings of self-esteem and imagination.

When the infant looks at herself in a mirror, she is aware that she is seeing herself. This can prove to be quite a delight when she tips the mirror to get a slightly different perspective. A mirror set up on the floor will certainly draw her attention as she learns to creep and crawl. She'll spend many moments examining, conversing, and playing with her reflected image.

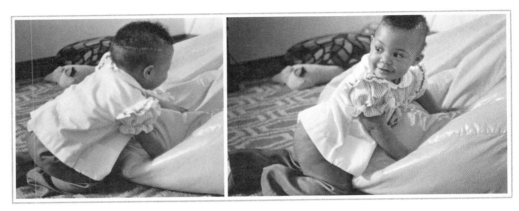

An indication of the infant's growing sense of herself as separate from others is her ability to respond to her own name. A first peek-a-boo game might involve simply calling the child's name when she's not looking at you. She'll turn toward you in response to her name, elated that you know who she is. This game can be repeated as she turns away once again.

The Question of Childcare

When your infant enters the Creeper-Crawler stage, you may find that *you* are entering a new stage of parenting. The infant is awake for more hours and can interact with a variety of people. Your own needs may be changing and this can lead to questions about childcare options. If you returned to work soon after the child was born, you have already considered the childcare issue. If, however, you have spent the greater part of the last four or five months caring for your infant, you may be feeling a desire for adult companionship outside the home. You may begin to feel some stir-craziness; you may even feel trapped. At the same time you may become keenly aware of the commitment you've made. There is a new person in your life who needs and depends on you and will continue to do so for many years to come.

It is very important, for both you and your infant, that you think seriously about your own needs. There is no hard and fast rule about how often to get out of the house or when to go back to work (if at all). What you need for your own sense of well-being and comfort will differ from what another person needs. But if you feel resentful, trapped, angry, desperate, or even just bored, you aren't doing your infant a favor by trying to live up to some myth of what an "ideal" parent should be. If you need to get out of the house, get out of the house! Making arrangements for time for yourself will require an extra bit of energy. Once the initial arrangements have been made, however, and you're free to shop, take a class, play cards, visit, dine out, work, or read, you'll probably return to your child with renewed energy and interest.

Although nearly sixty percent of the mothers in this country work outside the home, subsidized childcare is available for less than thirty percent. This means that the majority of working parents—and parents who just want time for themselves—are left to arrange and pay for childcare themselves. With all the other expenses of a baby, childcare may seem either impossible to afford or not worth the bother. Arranging for childcare, however, is a necessity for most parents,

at least occasionally, and it is worth the bother to find the best care possible for your child.

How do you go about this? First, consider your needs. How often do you need childcare and for how long? What kind of values, ideas, attitudes, practices do you look for in a caregiver? It is helpful to talk about this with other family members, other parents, and friends. You might even want to draw up a list of standards for these critical features of any childcare arrangement:

- Health/physical care
- Amount of interaction and attention the child will receive
- Personal warmth of the caregiver
- Physical surroundings

Second, find out what the resources are in your area. Shop around! If you are considering a day care center, spend a day or two there. Ask questions. Make sure you'll be allowed to visit when you wish. Find out how open they are to your ideas on raising a child.

If you prefer to have someone come into your home, you can ask some of the same questions. In addition, spend time in your home while the sitter is there, so you can see how she acts with the child. Give her information and suggestions about what your child likes or is interested in. Plan regular meetings with her and others who care for your child so you can find out what they are learning about your child; together you can make plans to support your child's development.

Feeding & Teething

The amount of time it takes to feed, bathe, and diaper will increase during the Creeper-Crawler stage simply because the baby will be much more willing and able to make these times playful. You may notice this particularly during feeding time. The infant is likely to interrupt feeding by trying to play a game, perhaps a simple form of hide-and-seek, perhaps exploring the spoon rather than eating from it. Or he might be distracted by other things happening in the room. He may suddenly stop eating and try to start a game, but this doesn't mean he is full and finished eating; nor does it mean he's a finicky eater. It doesn't mean he is dawdling. *It does mean that he's ready for a little play.* He has no understanding of the notion that meals should happen within a given length of time, or that mealtimes are only for eating. He is eager to be diverted from the task at hand. So make sure you allow more time for feeding.

It is during this stage that solid foods are introduced to the child, so a new dimension is added to feeding times. Some people now buy food mills and make their own babyfoods by pureeing meats, vegetables, and fruit. Many commercial babyfood producers are no longer adding synthetic chemicals to their products, so the babyfoods you buy in stores today may be of higher quality than they used to be.

Your child's willingness to try new foods and his attitude toward eating will be influenced by how you introduce these new solid foods. For example, introduce them when the feeding isn't rushed. Both you and the baby should be relaxed and comfortable and have time to learn about new foods.

The spoon should be small so that it fits the baby's mouth. The very first taste shouldn't be a mouthful. Let the baby explore the food just as he has been exploring everything else in his life. He'll probably enjoy the new smells, tastes, and textures. At first he may only move the food around with his tongue and not swallow it, but by the end of his first attempt, he'll probably have swallowed several small spoonfuls.

As the first solid food (generally a plain cereal) becomes a part of the infant's regular meals, you can begin to introduce greater variety. One good way of introducing foods with stronger tastes, such as vegetables, is to mix a small amount with the infant's cereal, to give him a preview of the new food. Children's stomachs tend to be sensitive at first, so avoid very spicy food. New foods should be introduced one at a time. That way if there is an allergic reaction, you'll know what is causing it.

This is also a wonderful time to introduce "finger foods": since the infant is now able to pick up small objects and put them in his mouth, foods like peas, and cut-up bananas become nutritious ways to practice dexterity.

Toward the end of this stage, your baby may attempt to feed himself. This will proceed by trial and error and will be messy, but the pleasure both of you will  take in the effort to bring spoon to mouth will probably outweigh the inconvenience to you. Be prepared for him to try eating his whole meal with his fingers when he gets frustrated with the spoon. You can put newspaper or a plastic cloth on the floor; this will make it easier for you to clean up after the meal. One mother avoided the inevitable mess by feeding her infant outdoors on nice days and hosing down the highchair afterwards. On inside days, she depended on the family dog to take care of spills on the kitchen floor.

It is also during this stage that the child begins teething. For some children this is a very painful process; others seem to cut teeth without a whimper. One sign that teething is beginning is a very fussy child who is chewing on every object he can get to his mouth. The pressure of chewing helps relieve some of the pain.

There are a number of items on the market that have been developed for sore gums. Plastic tubes—in the form of donuts and rattles—are filled with a liquid. Putting them in the refrigerator will make them cold. The cold feels good on the infant's tender gums as he chews the tube. The enclosed liquid is not always safe for children to swallow if the plastic tube comes open; check the description of the liquid on the container. Also, check to see that the plastic is well sealed so that no liquid escapes, and that it resists a sharp bite.

Favorite foods during teething are those which are more solid and dissolve slowly. An infant can make a piece of Zwieback last a long time.

Communication
Making sounds

As the infant becomes more of a social being, she shows more understanding of the reason for language. Since the Heads Up stage, she has been making noises, what we might call "babbling." She's been able to repeat her own sounds but has not been attempting to imitate the sounds of others. As she becomes more aware of others and attempts to play with them, she becomes aware that language is part of play. By the end of this stage, she is imitating the sounds she hears from adults—nothing complex, but recognizable to you.

Before the infant can make these recognizable sounds, she needs to hear them consistently. As you are doing things with her, talk to her about them. As she is exploring objects, describe for her what she is doing with them. "You opened the box. Can you close it?" Name the parts of her body during bathtime; make the sounds of animals she sees. Repeat the infant's sounds in a simple rhythmic pattern. As the infant watches you do things around the house, tell her what you are doing. "I'm going to wash the dishes." "I'll use the hammer to pound in the nail." You are giving her a way to begin to connect sounds with objects and events. She begins to see that they go together, and that she can let you know what she wants by giving you the right sounds, which eventually become words.

Choosing Toys

Here are some guidelines for choosing toys and objects that your infant might safely explore: (1) They should be sturdy. (2) They shouldn't have sharp edges or points. Smooth, rounded corners are much safer. (3) The infant should be able to handle an object with one hand since working with two hands is not a well developed skill at this stage. He should be able to grasp an object in more than one place. It should be light enough to be shaken and small enough not to knock the child over if he pulls on it. (4) Examine toys closely to make sure there are no detachable parts. Look out for button eyes not securely sewn on, tassels that can be pulled off, a part of a toy that could break off and leave an exposed nail. Do not *assume* that a toy is safe—even if it is made by a well-known toy manufacturer who presumably knows about safety issues. All too often there are newspaper stories about a toy that has been recalled because there were parts that infants have detached and swallowed. (5) Infants enjoy brightly colored objects, but be sure that the paint or dye will not come off.

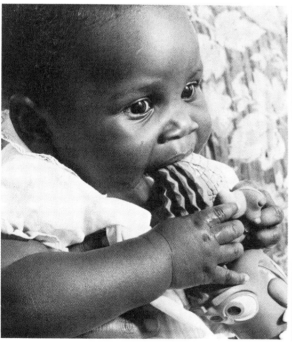

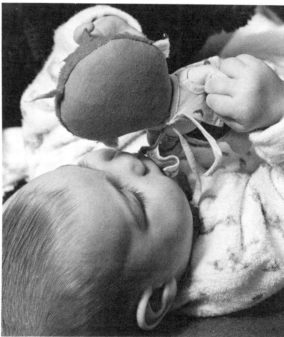

Understanding the World
More knowledge means more choices

The infant now understands more about her world. Her greater understanding enables her to choose what she is going to do in response to events and people. During earlier stages her actions were pretty much the same no matter what the situation, because she didn't have enough experience to know what was appropriate; she lacked the ability to choose how to respond. In thinking about what your infant is able to do in her world, consider what she understands and what that means she can do.

It may seem obvious to you that an object exists even when it isn't in sight, but this is something a child only gradually comes to understand. You might have noticed in your infant's first few months that her interest in an object lasted only as long as the object was in view. Even familiar objects, once out of sight, were forgotten. Now the infant begins to recognize a familiar object if only a part of it is in view. In other words, if a favorite toy is partially hidden, but a recognizable part of it remains in view, your infant will know what it is and go after it. Eventually, when she watches someone hide a favorite toy under a cloth, she can figure out that she can remove the cloth to get to the toy. She saw the toy disappear but knows it is still there.

Watch your Creeper-Crawler as he learns to make choices and responds to people and events in a variety of ways.

When placed on the floor in view of interesting objects, she is likely to try to reach for them. This motivates her to use her "creeping" muscles as well as her "reaching" ones. When she arrives at an object there are innumerable ways to explore it—she can roll, bang, squeeze, taste it, to mention just a few. With practice she can pass a cube or other small object from one hand to the other or pick up a cube in each hand. If you present her with a third object, she is stuck; she has to make a choice about what to hold on to and what to give up.

Your infant's understanding of how objects work is also expanding. For example, if a wind-up toy disappears behind the couch, the infant understands that the toy is in motion and that it will probably continue moving at the same pace; she begins to anticipate when the toy will reappear. She has come to understand that objects are separate and distinct from her—that they have, in a sense, a life of their own. This goes along with her understanding that *she* is separate and distinct and has a life of her own.

When the infant discovers that an action has a pleasing effect—kicking her

feet makes the mobile move, banging a toy on the table makes a pleasant sound, smiling can get someone to play peek-a-boo with her— she repeats the action. Although she still isn't quite aware of the con- nection between her action and the result, she will repeat the ac- tion as long as it produces the same result. She is not aware that by changing her action slightly she could modify the result—if she kicked the mobile harder it would move *and* make a noise. She is interested in reproducing the *same* result, not in experimenting to produce *new* results.

The Creeper-Crawler has two characteristics that appear to be in opposition. On the one hand, she can now be absorbed in an activity for as long as twenty or thirty minutes, either alone or with someone else. On the other hand, she is much more easily bored; she needs more stimulation—more interesting toys and objects to play with and more captivating things to see and do. It's really a question of *interest,* the touchstone of learning: when the infant is interested in exploring something, she will spend more time with it. But you won't be able to get away with constantly repeating the same activity— not unless *she* wants to repeat it. These characteristics will become more evident as the infant moves into the next stage.

Things to Do

Saving Energy

When the child is in the playpen or crib, or sitting in a highchair, her toys are likely to "fall overboard." You may find yourself constantly picking them up and returning them to her. Save your energy by tying toys to the chair and to the sides of the crib and playpen. That way when the toy "drops" it can be retrieved easily. At this stage, the child is unlikely to understand that she can get it back by pulling on a string, but after watching you do it often enough, she will begin to copy your actions.

Face-to-Face

The infant can now begin to understand who it is she sees in a mirror. This can prove to be quite a delight. As the infant is learning to scoot along, a mirror set up on the floor will draw her attention and get her moving. Tilt it to give her an added perspective. Offer the mirror when she is lying on her back, or sitting in her highchair. Prop it up in the playpen. She will have fun learning more about who she is from all these angles.

Stretching Those Creeper-Crawler Muscles

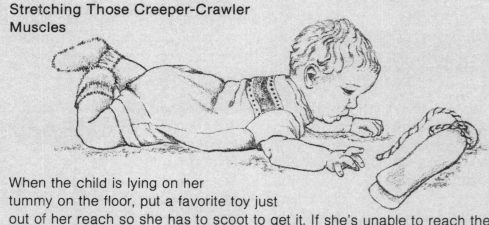

When the child is lying on her tummy on the floor, put a favorite toy just out of her reach so she has to scoot to get it. If she's unable to reach the toy, place it a little closer. As the child becomes more skilled at creeping and crawling, put the toy at a challenging distance—not so far away that she doesn't see it and would get exhausted going after it, but not so close that she doesn't have to stretch.

Talk, Talk, Talk

The infant loves to "talk." Using a real or a play phone, have a pretend conversation with the child. Hold the phone to your ear, then to hers. When she makes a sound, mimic it. Introduce a few sounds of your own. See if she will try to copy your sound. Talk to the child while doing things around the house—talk about what you are doing, give her names for the things you are using. She won't be able to repeat them back to you now, but she will begin to associate the sound of the word with the object. It won't be long before she will also give the object a name—although it might not be recognizable to everyone.

Bottom-Up Mobiles

Mobiles come in a variety of sizes and shapes and can be used in a number of ways. Many mobiles are made for adults. While you may think they are colorful, interesting, and attractive, the child may see only the uninteresting bottom—a circle, a wedge. So, when buying a mobile, look at it from the baby's point of view—bottom up! A mobile can be hung in the crib, attached to a playpen, some can even be put on the edge of a table. Place it where the infant can make it move with her hands and with her feet. Watch for her to discover that just wiggling and squirming can make the mobile move, too.

Playing Together

Begin an action game such as "pat-a-cake" by taking the infant's hands and going through the motions. Stop. Repeat the action. Stop again. This time wait for the baby's signal to begin the activity again—she might clap her hands, or reach for your hand to set it in motion.

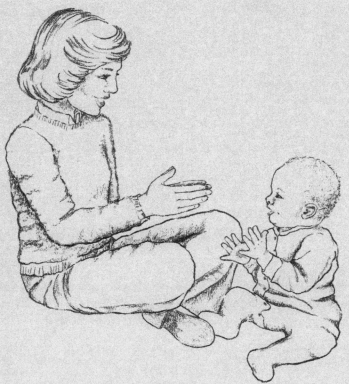

75

Chapter V

The Cruiser

"Cruising" refers to the infant's first attempts at traveling while standing, by holding on to furniture and pulling herself along. While this slows her down—crawling was faster— it does offer her a whole new world of places and things she can get into. She can now reach shelves, pull objects off tables, and topple chairs. This is a busy time of exploration for your infant, so prepare yourself.

By the time your infant enters the Cruiser stage, you will probably be used to having her underfoot. It should be a habit by now to pause before you open a door to make sure she isn't right on the other side. You can expect that when you move from room to room she'll tag along cheerfully, eager for attention.

During these months, it will feel like your infant is constantly doing something new. Some infants spend most of their time exploring things. They may especially enjoy dropping, throwing, picking up, and banging objects. Others seem to put most of their energy into moving about—taking those first few "cruising" steps and practicing standing and sitting. Still other infants appear to be most fascinated by other people. Every situation becomes a game, whether you want it to or not. The noise level in the house rises as the child busily tries out sounds, imitates you and others,

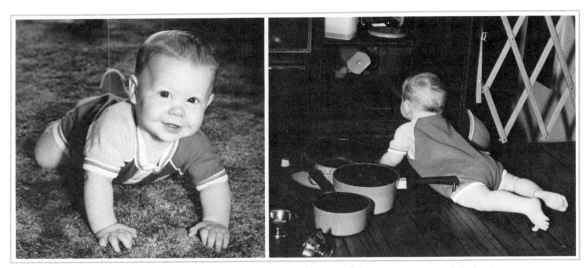

The child's ability to think is expanding as his awareness of his body, surroundings, and actions expands. At this stage, the child is moving about, exploring, playing games with and imitating those persons closest to him.

and tries to get you to imitate her. Most infants will be doing all of these things to some extent. Take a few minutes every now and then to ask yourself what *your* child is focusing on now.

Infants learn in different ways. Many stumble on a new skill by trial and error and then practice it by the hour. Others appear to be paying little attention, and then suddenly they are able to use a new skill. Some can be seen carefully watching siblings or parents doing something, and then they imitate, skipping the discover-it-yourself step. How does *your* infant learn? The way your infant learns is partially determined by her environment. If there are older sisters and brothers, chances are she will learn at least some skills by imitating them. Other children can play an important part in "motivating" the infant: the social aspects of the situation are usually as rewarding as learning the new skill itself. If, on the other hand, your infant is a first or only child, she may do a great deal more watching and exploring. But each person is different. Observe your infant closely; your role in helping her learn new things will depend upon her particular personality, as *you* see it and respond to it.

Sometimes, it is hard to know how to respond to the infant's on-again, off-again independence. She needs freedom to make mistakes, but you should step in when frustrations are great.

In some ways your infant is more independent now. She seeks out things to amuse herself. When given interesting objects and toys, or a place to practice a new skill, she can spend more time alone without being bored. On the other hand, her activities do require support from you in many ways.

Since your infant is experiencing growth spurts—physical *and* mental— there may be times when she will cling to you, letting you know she needs to be reassured. This is a natural reaction. Even adults need to be reassured when they are doing something new or taking risks. Your child will use familiar people, especially you, as a home base, a center of

security. This may mean calling to you from another room, or crawling about to find you. Often your infant will need to be helped out of a jam. For example, she might start to climb the stairs, get stuck and scared, and cry to be rescued. After you carry her down and give her a reassuring hug she might crawl right back up the stairs, turning your rescue attempt into a game. When she first figures out how to stand she may have trouble sitting again without falling. She may call you repeatedly to help her sit down. She'll need your assistance until she's comfortable doing it on her own.

Physical Abilities
Standing up to be counted

Your infant may grow quickly or slowly. She may be an early walker, or she may not even attempt to walk for months. She may start picking up objects and dropping them with great skill while she can barely crawl. Not all cruisers will show all of the abilities described in this chapter. And not all infants who can drop and throw, or who can see a link between actions and reactions, will be able to cruise. This makes your job tougher. You will need to pay careful attention to what your baby can do, and support her in that. No book on children's development can predict the speed or the focus of your child's growth at any given time. We can only suggest what to look for, and how to make the most of what you see.

Your child will begin developing physical skills when her body is ready, *and* when she is encouraged and challenged by the people in her life.

You play an important role in helping your infant learn how to use her body. Consider the following example:

Georgie discovered how to pull himself up to a standing position using the edge of the couch. He also found that if he let go, he would fall back down, and if he bent at the middle, he would end up sitting. Now, instead of crawling around after his sister, he would spend as much time as he could practicing this new trick. At first he was shaky, and even someone calling

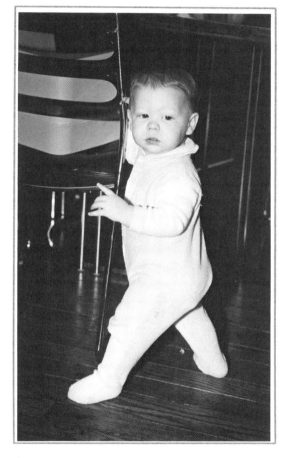

to him would cause him to lose his balance and fall over backward. Eventually, though, he could turn his head and look at people as they entered the room. Georgie's father noticed that Georgie was learning, and kept himself in the background for a while, not wanting to interrupt Georgie's practice. But once his son was a little more solid on his feet and would stand up at every opportunity, Georgie's father would sit on the couch a few feet away, to see if his son would try to work his way over to him. Sure enough, when his father talked to him, Georgie would begin to inch his way over. When Georgie got within a foot or so of him, his father would whisk him up and swing him around in the air, to the delight of both of them. It became their favorite game, and soon Georgie was cruising over to his father, with increasing coordination, whenever his father sat down.

Standing and cruising are new accomplishments for your infant. Not only does she have to strengthen all the muscles involved, but she also has to learn a new kind of balance. When she is standing, she is orienting herself to a new position in space: things look different and feel different. At first, just standing (holding on to furniture) is a feat, and almost any disturbance can topple her. But soon she's more steady. She experiments with turning her head to look at something. She also learns to turn the upper part of her body.

As she practices cruising, your infant is learning to alternate hands for holding on, and to alternate lifting and moving her feet. She learns that with her free hand she can reach for toys or other objects that interest her. At first this reaching may topple her, but once she's managed it, a range of new activities is open to her.

As she includes other goals in her cruising, such as cruising down to the end of the couch to get a toy that she sees, your infant will also be ready to do some more complicated things while standing: bending to different sides (still holding on to the couch), stooping down to reach something that has fallen on the floor (as opposed to sitting down to pick it up, then standing again), and squatting. Cruising is still a new skill, however, so your infant will probably rely heavily on crawling when she wants to get around fast.

Most of this is work your infant has to do on her own. You can encourage her by being there, ready to provide a hand at the elbow as she

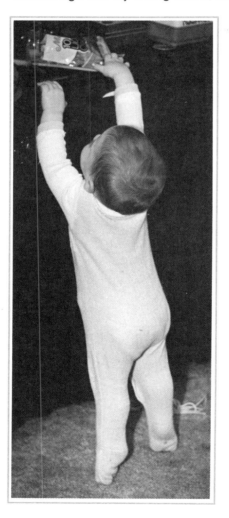

Your child is learning to choose what she wants to play with and her developing physical skills allow her to carry out her choice.

begins to topple, or to steady the chair she's holding on to so she doesn't pull it down on top of herself. And like Georgie's father, you can help your infant learn new skills by giving her opportunities to use them as the two of you play.

One of the new skills she will learn is to let go of an object intentionally. This opens up many possibilities. Not only is there an interesting sound as the object hits the floor, but a moving object is also interesting to watch. The infant's repertoire of things to do with an object expands from tasting, touching, and looking to banging, turning, shaking, dropping, and eventually throwing. To adults, these additions can be exasperating. If you have feeding in mind, and the infant has dropping, it can be a battle of wills. So give your child opportunities to throw and drop objects at other times, to allow her plenty of playing time to practice this new skill. She's excited about what she has learned. She is exploring and expanding her skill, and if you can take it in that spirit, it's easier to handle.

Now that she can pick up objects and

put them down again, your infant can choose more actively what she wants to play with next. She'll be able to crawl to get an object that she has spied across the room. This new ability to go after something shows many things about the way she is growing, mentally as well as physically. Upon seeing a toy she sets a goal for herself: *get it*. Then she goes after it. She has to keep the toy in mind and remember her goal while going after it. She's able to get to it without thinking about how to crawl; crawling is second nature to her now and allows her to do other things she has set her mind on.

Infants carry objects in different ways. Some put an object in their mouth and carry it dog style. Others differentiate between their hands, using one for holding and carrying, the other for reaching and exploring. The infant learns to transfer an object from one hand to another and can spend a long time moving objects from one place to another and filling and emptying containers.

Whenever she has the opportunity, your child will continue her exploration of her body and of the sensations it produces. Some infants learn to pull off socks and loosen blankets or other covers, then delight in discovering themselves beneath them. Your infant will probably discover her navel, and perhaps pull on it. Girls discover their clitoris and vagina and will play with themselves, much as boys do with their penises. This exploration is natural; if you regard it as natural, you will help your infant develop a healthy sense of her own body.

After a long and busy day of practicing new skills and getting into everything, you might expect your infant to be exhausted; *you* will be! Sometimes, though, her system carries on at night, as if it were a motor idling high. Some infants will rock in their crib, causing it to travel across the room or creak ominously. While this is not harmful, it can be annoying. This inability to slow down frequently accompanies spurts of growth. If your infant can't seem to stop at night, you have to take special care to help her wind down—rock her, pat her tummy, rub her back, sing to her.

Saying No & Setting Limits

It's important for you to think about how your role is changing at this time, because it *is* changing. Now, in addition to being a supporter and provider, you'll be expected to *react*. Sometimes when your infant drops his food or pulls your hair, he does it out of curiosity: what will happen? At other times he is trying to get you involved in a game. If he wants to play but the game is inconvenient for you, you can handle the situation by redirecting his interest. For example, if you're feeding him and he begins to drop food on the floor, you can remove his food and give him some clothespins he can drop in a container. At other times you won't have time to play, and *no* may be the best response. Remember that the child is not deliberately trying to annoy you. Understanding what the child wants may help you to react warmly, calmly, and playfully. But you need to set limits based on your own breaking point and to feel comfortable saying "No" firmly when you really have had enough.

If *no* is not over-used or used arbitrarily, it will be more effective. If you find yourself using it frequently, stop to look at how and when you're using it. Often in our fear for the child's safety, and in our frustration with his poking and getting into everything (not to mention his tendency to turn everything into a game), we use *no* to try to restrict his behavior. Instead, try to think ahead. If the child is about to grab something valuable, substituting a favorite object can satisfy him where screaming "No!" and slapping his hand would confuse him. If the child wants to drop his spoon rather than use it to eat with, letting him play for a while and then firmly ending the game (by, for example, taking the spoon away and letting him eat with his hands), will do more than yanking the spoon away from him and making him sit there while you spoon-feed him. In trying to find ways to cut down on the *no's,* consider the child's mood and what he is interested in. If, for example, you want him to calm down so you can feed him, and he seems to be winding up, a quiet activity like telling or reading a story would be a good transition.

There are times when you need to set firm limits for the infant's safety and sense of security, and for your sanity as well. Bedtime is a good example. If the child is allowed to stay up until he winds down (something many children are unable to do without help), he may well feel abandoned. But if you establish a bedtime routine he enjoys, he'll have the support he needs from you to learn to wind down. Not everything the child wants is good for him, and since he can't predict the consequences, it's up to you to help him.

Understanding the World
"What happens if. . ."

In earlier stages, the infant's actions were random, or in response to an object, face, or situation. But now she begins to initiate actions. She sees the results of actions and then tries things out to see what else might happen. Her attitude becomes, "What happens if. . .?" "What happens if I bang the block? What happens if I bang the pillow? What happens if I drop my food? What happens if I throw my shoe?" You can see on her face the concentration and the delight—she is watching to see what she has caused.

The infant learns to achieve a goal by repeating or varying some action she's tried in the past. She remembers the splendid noise she got when she banged the block on the floor, and instead of merely repeating the same action, she might try banging the block on a can.

You can see her listening to the noise she gets with her new action.

At first she is just trying out possibilities: she tugs at a tablecloth and the dishes fall off the table; she tugs on a string and an attached toy duck waddles toward her. After a while she begins to remember the results of her actions; she can remember the noise the spoon made when she dropped it from her highchair, and she'll drop her spoon just to hear the noise.

Eventually your infant will be able to come up with a mental plan: she will see something she desires and figure out a way to get it. For example, she may see a block she wants on a blanket. If she's had enough experience with tugging on the blanket, she'll be able to figure out that she can pull on the blanket in order to get the block.

The infant's understanding of time is developing rapidly. Now, when she drops her spoon, she may blink in anticipation of the sound it will make when it hits the floor. This shows that she remembers what will happen and has a sense of how long it will take.

The infant learns to hold several things in mind at once. If she decides she wants to play in the room where her mother is, she can keep that in

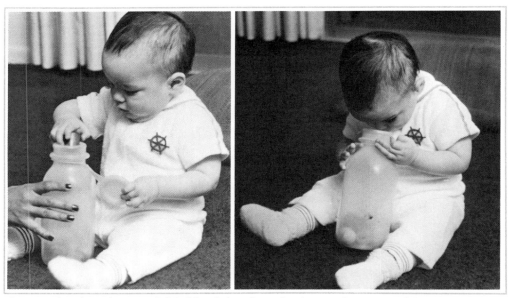

One of the first signs of "thinking" is when the infant does something on purpose, in order to see what will happen.

mind while transporting her toys, one by one, to the new location. Or, if she's trying to crawl to greet her father and there's a couch in the way, she can try to find a way around the couch and still remember her original errand. This is a tremendous accomplishment—the infant is using her knowledge of the world around her to actively solve problems.

Your infant is probably beginning to recognize an object even if most of it is hidden. For example, if you cover a favorite toy most of the way with a blanket, she can still recognize it and go after it. Peek-a-boo games are very popular at this stage.

The infant is starting to understand something about the position of objects in space. When she reaches up to grasp an object, she learns to turn her hand at the correct angle in order to grasp it without fumbling. If she watches you hiding a block under a scarf, she can remember to look for the block. If she sees a ball rolling behind the couch, she knows to look toward the other end of the couch for the ball to emerge. But if the block is not under the scarf, or if the ball doesn't emerge, the child doesn't have enough of an understanding of objects to figure out what happened. For her, the ball and the block no longer exist.

Her experience with standing and being upright makes her more aware of heights. Now she is likely to have fears she didn't have earlier: fears of falling, of heights, of being playfully tossed in the air. She will experiment with looking at things from different viewpoints, turning herself around to change perspective.

Your infant is beginning to imitate others, and in so doing she will learn from them. If you listen closely to her babbling now, she'll sound almost as if she were conversing! She can imitate your tones and cadences even if the syllables are nonsense. She can also imitate simple actions, such as wiping off her tray. She may associate actions with familiar objects. For example, if a telephone is within her reach, she may pick it up and "talk on the telephone." This is the beginning of role play.

Dangers

The infant can reach higher now, so anything not meant for his hands should be stored above where you think he can reach. He also gets around more, and behind and into unexpected places. Tablecloths or electrical cords are prime targets for those busy hands; he can easily pull them, bringing down not only the dishes or the attached appliance, but sometimes even the table itself. Chests, laundry bins, closets, and old refrigerators can all be dangerous traps for an infant who can bumble his way in but not get himself out. Even stairs can be a danger: the child learns first to climb up stairs; learning to get down comes later. A more patient infant will cry for help. A less patient infant may opt for the quick way and fall. Many household items are poison for children. A few of the most common ones are listed here. In addition, electrical outlets should be covered or barricaded so curious fingers can't touch them. In-floor heating vents, especially the older furnace-in-floor types, should be blocked by furniture. Hot radiators, too, should be blocked off. Glass items, including knicknacks and bottles, should be placed not only out of reach, but also where a good shake from below can't topple them off shelves or tables. Take a tour around your house to make sure it's baby-proofed. Survey each room from your knees so you can see it from the infant's perspective. Is there anything below the four-foot level that you could pull over, get your hands on, break, or wreck?

Poisons Commonly Found About the House

Ammonia	Lighter fluid
Aspirin	Metal polish
Bathroom cleansers	Paint
Bleach	Paint thinner
Contraceptive pills	Perfume
Deodorants	Permanent-wave
Depilatories	solutions
Detergents	Rat poison
Diuretics	Reducing pills
Drain cleaner	Room deodorizer
Fabric softener	Rubbing alcohol
Floor wax	Rug cleaner
Glue	Shampoo
Hairspray	Shoe polish
Headache remedies	Sleeping pills
Heart medicines	Tranquilizers
Insecticides	Turpentine
Iodine	Varnish
Kerosene	Vitamins
Laxatives	Washing soda

Sense of Self
Expressing feelings

Depending on their temperament and environment, infants will adjust to their growing awareness of the world in different ways. Does your infant tend to put all her energy into crawling or cruising or does she tend to spend her time sitting and playing with objects—dropping, banging, shaking them to see what will happen? Does she tend to perk up when others are in the room with her, or does she become shy and helpless?

Your infant's emotional adjustments will depend on her temperament, and also on the ways open for her to express herself. She will do what she can to express her needs and feelings. It's important for you to look beyond her difficult behavior—crying, crawling near a dangerous place, babbling loudly and insistently, throwing objects, rocking, fondling herself—to the causes or meaning of the behavior. You don't have to be an amateur psychologist, but you will occasionally have to ignore your initial reaction to what the child is *doing,* in order to figure out what she's trying to *say* through her actions. Is she bored and trying to get your attention in order to play a game? Is she overtired? Is she frustrated because she doesn't have enough time with an object before someone takes it away? Is she reacting to taking new risks (such as attempts to stand) with fear? Is she trying, and perhaps failing, to understand what you mean when you say no? Is she exploring or comforting herself? Is she reflecting some tensions in

the household you might not have thought she'd perceive?

Some infants at this stage become fearful and begin to cling as a reaction to taking more risks. Other infants may plunge headlong into independence and resent being cuddled when they are working on some new problem. For others, being weaned may be a kind of symbol of their independence; they may not experiment with crawling and cruising *until* they've been weaned.

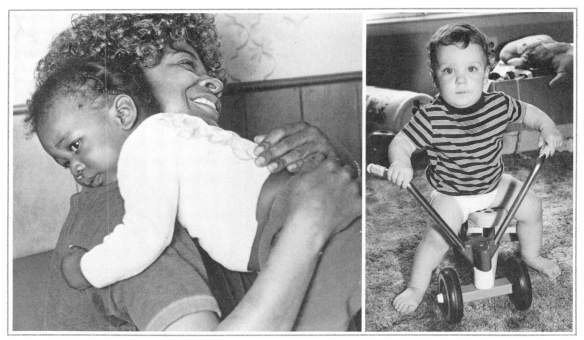

As they grow, infants become more aware of the world around them and the people in it. They begin making their own emotional adjustments, but still need your guidance and understanding.

This is the stage in which many infants demonstrate a sense of humor, turning their mistakes into games. An infant may, for example, drop her toy, hear the noise it makes as it hits the floor, look startled, then break into a broad grin and drop it again excitedly as soon as it's returned to her. Having invented a new game, she'll play it as long as you're willing to continue.

Your infant may begin to express herself more purposefully now, showing a wide range of feelings—calling out to you with joyful shrieks, being aloof with one household member and affectionate with another. She may show tenderness by "mothering" a favorite toy or a blanket or a shoe. It's a good idea to let her drag the object of her affections around with her as she goes about her day; this may furnish her with just enough security to enable her to concentrate on all the learning she's trying to do.

Relationships
Spending time together

Your infant's explorations will require a new resourcefulness on your part. She'll need not only a variety of *things* to play with, but also a variety of games she can play *with you.* If you are used to spending time with your infant, these new games can grow naturally out of the relationship. They needn't be fancy; just use the child's natural curiosity, the objects around you, and your imagination. You don't need to set up special activities. Just get in the habit of picking up on games your infant starts and introducing games you think she would enjoy.

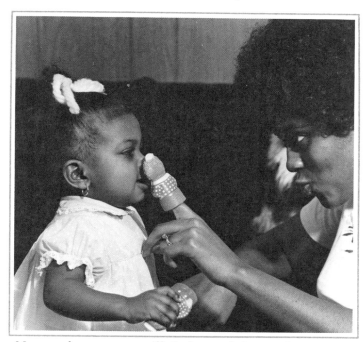

More and more, you will find your infant trying to start games, to catch your attention, to get you and other household members involved with her.

Because your infant is physically more independent, it's easy to forget that the intimate times you spend together are still important for both of you. Bathtime may have become more of a playtime, but afterwards there's also opportunity to wrap the child in a towel and spend some quiet moments together, perhaps singing, reading a story, breast- or bottle-feeding, or just talking quietly. You can use quieter activities to help your infant make transitions—from playtime to mealtime, from mealtime to naptime, from evening play to bedtime.

You should set definite, consistent limits, and have regular routines for transitions to bedtime, bathtime, and feeding time which are firm (but not rigid) and fair. Bedtime, bathtime, and naptime should be at regular intervals; they should begin with a procedure the infant can count on (a warning that bedtime is coming, a "calm-down" story, then the tucking in). If the infant senses limits aren't serious, she'll begin to feel anxious.

Frustration

To an adult mind, the repeated attempts an infant has to make in order to accomplish the simplest action can seem like an exercise in frustration. It is tempting to want to do things for him. At times the child may be grateful for your help. At other times your help may compound his frustration. There's a thin line between being helpful and intruding, and a quieter infant may not let you know immediately if you are intruding. It may come out later as fussiness around bedtime, or a refusal to eat solid foods.

Try to see both frustration and satisfaction from your infant's point of view. Learning patience, and learning to try even if he's failed in the past, is important for the infant, no matter how painful it may appear to you. Remember also that a house full of restrictions and arbitrary rules is a very frustrating place for an infant. Since learning the difference between what is and is not permitted is important for the child's safety (*don't* touch the stove, *do* enjoy banging your toy), limit your use of *no* to times when it's really necessary. A good general rule to keep in mind is, "Let him try it if it's safe."

When you need to set limits during transition times, beware of falling into the trap of using bribes, especially food. Instead, let the child know, by words, gestures, and touch, what is expected. Inevitably, your child will test the limits—she'll fuss when brought to the table, squirm when being bathed, and so on. But she expects you to hold to your routines, and will be disappointed if you don't.

Often, limits should be set because there is a safety issue at stake. For example, if your child tries to climb over the side of her crib and is in danger of falling out, you'll need to set a limit. If there's a hot stove and the baby keeps crawling toward it, you'll have to find a way to stop her. If it's possible to teach your infant to "solve the problem" (to sit down again in her crib), or if you can set up physical barriers (a secure gate at the top of stairs), this is certainly better than physically restricting her (keeping her in a playpen most of the time) or constantly scolding her.

Your child now understands many things about her environment, but this understanding isn't too secure yet. It's important, therefore, to avoid big changes. Changing your appearance—a new haircut—can upset her. Leaving her unexpectedly while you go on vacation can cause her to hold back on making discoveries and cling to some adult; even breaks in her daily routine, such as an unexpected visit by a friend, can cause fussiness or shyness. Sometimes, though, changes can't be avoided. In these cases, explain what is happening or about to happen, and reassure her with hugs and with a gentle tone of voice. Even though your infant won't understand all the words, she *will* understand your intention to reassure her. She'll still have a period of reaction to the change, but the trust you have established will help her to weather the emotional storm.

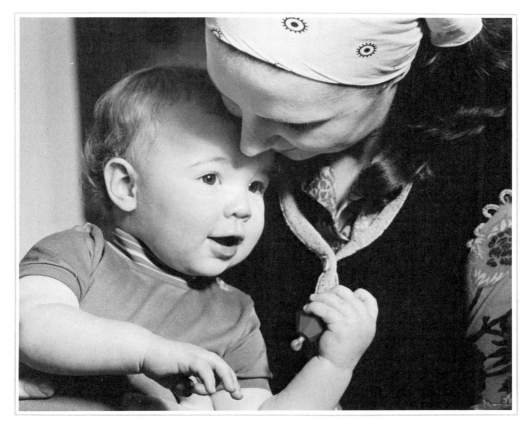

This growing, busy person is also still an infant and still needs plenty of nurturing from you.

Young children identify with each other, and your infant will be very interested in anything an older brother or sister does. Their actions will be quickly imitated, for better or worse. There are likely to be sibling rivalries. It's important to let siblings work out solutions to their problems as much as possible, but there are times when you'll need to step in. Siblings can play an important role in caring for (feeding, pushing in a stroller, dressing) and playing with the infant, provided they are under your guidance.

Throughout this period of rapid social development of your infant, you'll be having emotions of your own to contend with. You may feel rejected when the infant seems able to accept things from others (especially siblings) that she can't accept from you. You may feel at a loss when she is weaned—but the loss will soon be compensated by her growing ability to express affection for you.

Communication
Babbling, naming, joining in

By the time a child has reached the Cruiser stage, she is generally quite a babbler. If you've been talking to her all along and encouraging her to make sounds, the babbling is now likely to be a regular part of every activity.

Infants love to have their sounds repeated back to them, and at some point, they begin to imitate the sounds they hear. Their imitations eventually take on the inflections and cadence of human speech. The infant shows that she recognizes the "purpose" of language, babbling to her toys and blanket, calling out to you when you're in another room. Eventually she links gestures and facial expressions to her babbling. If adults are conversing, she'll often join in; while this can be annoying, it's important to give infants plenty of opportunity to talk. You'll probably find yourself developing the ability to carry on two conversations at once, responding to the infant now and then while still carrying on an adult conversation.

One of the first words the infant learns to understand is *no.* She may turn her understanding into a game, crawling toward forbidden objects shaking her head or muttering "No!" She's not, of course, being defiant, only acting out the meaning of a highly significant word.

You help the child understand the meaning of words when you name objects and actions for her. For example, if your infant points to her shoe and makes a sound, repeat the sound and add, "That's your shoe." Eventually the child will understand simple commands: "There's your shoe. Get me your shoe so we can put it on." A favorite of all infants is a point-

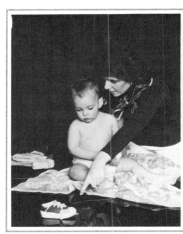

ing game in which the child points to objects and the adult names them. Eventually the roles can be reversed, with the adult pointing to objects and the child naming them. Sometimes a child will *seem* to have very little interest in speech, and then quickly learn to speak as if she had been practicing all along. If your child is babbling, it is communication. If your

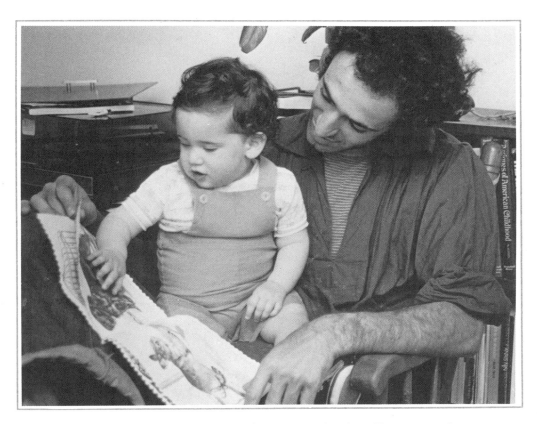

child is pointing or gesturing, it is still communication. Try as much as possible to respond to your child's sounds and gestures, letting her know you value her attempts to communicate.

During the Cruiser stage you've seen an increase in activity. Your child is now able to do more of what she wants to do; she can get to places she never could before. She can even think about what she wants to do and get it done, more or less. She's more responsive to things you say to her; she is beginning to understand the meaning of words, phrases, and certainly the tone of your voice. She is also becoming aware that she is a person in her own right, and she'll continue to try to understand what that means. All of these emerging characteristics will become even more evident as the child enters the Walker stage.

Things to Do

String Along

Now, your child can begin to use a string to get what she wants. When the child is on the floor, put a favorite toy across the room, but attach it to a string that you give to the child. If she doesn't make the connection between the string and the toy, give the string a tug so that she sees that pulling on the string will bring the toy closer. When she has made this connection, tie a string on a toy that the child cannot see (put the object in a box, or behind a chair). Encourage her to pull on the string to discover what is on the other end.

Names, Names, Names

Conversation picks up at this stage. The child is beginning to associate a name with an object. When the child is playing with her toys, ask her to give you the "truck," the "doll," the "cup." If she doesn't understand, show her, then ask for the same thing again. Your child will enjoy learning the names of body parts, too, especially on the face. Prop her up by a mirror and while she is watching herself, ask her to show you where her mouth is, her eyes, her ears, her nose, her chin. Move her hands to parts of her body while you say the names. After some practice, she will begin to do this on her own.

Ingenuity and Small-Muscle Control

Give your child several containers with interesting lids, covers, and fasteners. Let the child watch you put a toy in each container and encourage the child to find the best way to open each one. Use a screw-top jar, snap-open coin purse, cigar box, bandage box, and any other *safe* containers that the child is capable of opening.

Practicing Cruising

Stand the child next to the couch and encourage her to inch her way along to get a favorite toy at the other end.

Sizing Things Up

Separate four measuring cups that can be stacked together. Let the child play with them, exploring how they go together. As the child explores the cups, she will learn that if you put the smallest cup in the biggest cup, there is no room for the others. See if she can solve this problem herself. If she seems frustrated, take away one of the cups. Show her how to put three of the cups together, then see if she can do it. Gradually work up to using all four cups. Another toy that can be used for this activity is a cone-shaped post that has different sized rings which slip over it.

Follow the Leader

Your child will be absolutely delighted if you can turn whatever she is doing into a game. As she claps her hands, do the same, perhaps adding a rhyme to go along with the action. If she bangs her hand on the table, give her something to bang that makes a different noise—perhaps a spatula or the lid of a pan. Be quick in your responses to your child's cues. Unless you respond quickly, your child will lose interest and turn to another activity.

Take Me Out to the Ball Game

Balls of various sizes offer a variety of activities for you and your child. She can grasp a ball with two hands, attempt to throw it to you, or scoot after it when you roll it to her. One way to "play ball" is to have her sitting on the floor with her legs apart. Roll the ball between her legs, encouraging her to roll it back to you. You may need to retrieve the ball for her several times until she gets the idea. For another ball game, roll a ball slightly out of your child's reach so that she has to go after it. If it's thrown too far away she may lose interest and decide to play with something else. At this stage, the child doesn't have enough force to do much damage with her "throw," so games can be played inside if the ball is soft enough. However, this is a good out-of-doors activity, if the weather permits.

Chapter VI

We are used to thinking about a child's development in terms of "firsts." We talk about the first time she sits up by herself, the first time she reaches out to grab hold of a toy, the first syllable she repeats, the first time she walks by herself. The Walker stage is characterized by some important firsts: the infant takes her first steps on her own, begins to recognize and use words, learns to assert her own will.

The Walker

These firsts are, of course, very significant. But they are not the whole story. Think about your first day at a job. It was certainly important, but the days which followed were equally important. You probably had to learn new skills, to perfect old ones, to become more efficient, to adjust emotionally to the drudgery or excitement of the job, to adjust physically to the demands on your energy. In the same way, your child's *day to day* experiences are the raw material of her growth.

Physical Abilities
Walking

Each child has her own way of learning to walk. Some children practice balancing for a long time before they take that first step. Others are up and off in a matter of hours. Whatever the case, walking is of course a major landmark in a child's development.

To be able to walk, the child must first be able to stand alone. Learning to stand without support is no easy task. It means learning to balance. This is rarely accomplished without plenty of false starts and falls. Almost anything can topple the child at first: fear of disturbance from siblings, loud noises, sudden movements. Like any other balancing act, standing up alone requires concentration. But even under less than ideal circumstances, almost all children do manage sooner or later to accomplish this feat. They show tremendous persistence.

What your child needs most, in order to get and keep himself upright, is practice time.

Your child will eventually learn to turn and twist while still keeping his balance.
He will learn to stoop down and pick up a toy or other object that interests him.

Walking while holding on to an adult's arms and cruising both help children learn to balance. In addition, many children have walkers and other equipment to support them as they begin to walk.

When your child learns to balance, she may be so thrilled with standing that she won't want to sit. Often when you try to put her in her highchair, the tub, her crib or stroller, she will insist on standing. Most Walkers very determinedly stiffen their legs; it's a struggle to get them to sit or lie down. Since this is a perfectly natural development, you will have to be open to alternatives. Can you change her diaper while she stands at the couch? Can you soap or rinse her as she holds on to the side of the tub?

Stairs will be a temptation to the child. She'll be able to climb up before she learns how to come down. Until she has developed the skill of going up *and* down (she can practice this when you're nearby), stairwells should be blocked. There are many household items and toys that infants can make good use of during this stage, such as sturdy pushtoys with long handles, large springy pillows (these can be made with scrap material), a chair turned on its side as a combination walker and pushcart.

She may get into the habit of following you around the house, making sure she's at the center of things. After a couple of months of practice, she'll be able to climb onto chairs, the kitchen table, slides and swings, as well as amuse herself bouncing on furniture.

By this stage the child has become skillful at grasping and handling objects. She learns to combine her new stooping and grasping skills to pick up small objects (even pieces of lint). She can use a crayon to scribble. She can tear (as well as crumple) paper, coordinating both hands in the action. She learns to imitate complex motions. She can also balance one block on another to make a tower, take lids off containers, and open packages.

Support-ing Your Child's Learning

How can you support your child's learning as he plays with familiar toys or repeats favorite activities? First of all, allow him the time and freedom to experiment with objects and develop his skills. Follow his lead. If he finds a quiet area to practice his cruising or pile blocks and knock them over, your role at first should probably be that of observer. Does he vary his actions at all? Does he appear to have a definite idea in mind of what to do with his toy, or is he poking and pushing at it to see what will happen? When something happens accidentally, how does he react? Does he try to make the accident happen again or stick to what he was doing before?

When you notice your child doing something new, either accidentally or on purpose, you can support him. For example, if he knocks over a block structure by mistake, try building another tower that he can knock down, making the "mistake" into a game.

You can also introduce a new game or a new way of using a toy, if it fits in with what your child is doing. For example, a child who has discovered how to put rings on a peg and does it over and over might enjoy it if you showed him how to turn the peg sideways and roll it on the floor. If he isn't interested, he'll let you know. If he is, he'll make it a part of his game.

What is your child learning when he plays with his food? Is he learning to use his thumb and forefinger together? Is he exploring a new texture? Is he practicing picking up and putting down? Or is he trying to assert his will by stalling? Your response to his actions should depend on *why* he is playing with his food. If it's exploration, then you might let him continue, even if it causes some inconvenience. If it's a statement of individuality ("No, I won't eat now"), then you'll need to find a way

to defuse the situation so that he can assert his independence but also get some food into his stomach.

Understanding the World
Practicing, experimenting, imitating

By the time your child enters the Walker stage, she has gained a certain amount of control over the familiar objects around her. She has learned that she can drop her spoon and get a satisfying sound, that she can push her tennis ball and make it roll, that she can shake a can of dried beans and hear great noises. Now she'll want to perform variations on these themes: throw her spoon, roll the can of beans.

Your child may repeat the same activity over and over, or play with the same toy day in and day out. If adults do this we tend to think they aren't learning much. But for children, it's a very different story. Your child is learning to master objects physically, and to create a picture of an object in her mind. This in itself takes hours of practice. She takes in all kinds of information about an object, about her actions on or with the object, and about the results of her actions. The information she takes in affects, and is affected by, what she already knows. She experiences sensations (hot, cold, fuzzy, rough) and learns to distinguish between them, to compare and contrast hot and cold, fuzzy and rough. She becomes an experimenter, testing how the same action has different results with different objects. She finds that banging a block produces a noise, banging a piece of banana produces a mess, and banging a brother produces a bang in return.

The Walker is developing an overall picture of the shape and makeup of her environment. When she enters a room, she is able to survey the scene and make a choice of where to go and what to explore. She becomes more skilled in moving about, and in using her hands. She learns to make things work—pushing and pulling, emptying cupboards, poking into shelves and drawers, zipping zippers, taking lids off pots and pans.

She begins to understand the concept of inside/outside, learning that she can put objects inside a container and take them out again. She can put a smaller bowl into a larger one, and can drop beans into a plastic carton, making a very satisfying plunk each time. She can put a peg into a hole and pull it out again. She learns to open containers and pour out their contents. She experiments with pulling (using pull toys or pulling on a string to which something is attached). Days and weeks of experimenting will begin when she discovers that she can use an object as a tool . . . that she can *get something* with it. More and more she is coming to "possess" the objects of her world, through knowledge born of action.

The child's range of exploration expands, and his understanding of objects is more complete. The child not only is learning that objects exist regardless of where they are found, but also about how they work.

Imitation is a form of action that takes on increasing significance during the Walker stage. The child will of course be imitating things she sees people doing—repeated actions such as wiping off a tray, sweeping the floor, or petting the cat. But soon she'll be imitating these actions *after* they've taken place. For instance, when you're not around she might pick up a brush and brush her hair, just like you. Or she might cradle a stuffed toy, then shake her head and give a stern "No," imitating what she herself has experienced. She is demonstrating a memory for actions she's seen before and an awareness of actions and words appropriate to particular objects. These are giant steps in early thinking and reasoning.

Establishing a Routine for the Walker

Each household will have its own routine, depending on the schedule and needs of the family members. There is no "best" routine but here are some questions to consider in deciding what kind of schedule you want to set for your child.

What is the best sleeping schedule for your child, and does it mesh with the availability of other family members? For example, does he nap once or twice a day? Is he able to fall asleep anywhere, or does he need to be in a familiar setting before falling asleep? If he goes to sleep at 7 p.m. for the night, does he miss seeing other people who are important in his life? If so, perhaps he could take a short nap in the afternoon and then stay awake longer in the evening, which would give him a chance to be with other family members.

When, what, and how much is your child expected to eat? How much "play" (with food, people, utensils) are you comfortable with at mealtimes? How much time will you spend playing with your child, and how much time is he expected to spend playing by himself (with supervision, of course)? How do you prepare your child to face transitions (from playtime to mealtime, from playtime to naptime, from being awake to going to bed at night, from one activity to another)?

Communication
Beginning to talk

Although the following discussion focuses on language learning, don't forget the importance of the nonverbal communication that goes on between you and your child. Patting your child, giving her a quick hug, holding her on your lap, cuddling her, sharing activities such as eating (a bite for you, a bite for me), making faces and gestures are all important ways of communicating with her.

In the Walker stage, the child's language abilities become more and more evident, not only what she is able to say, but particularly in her growing ability to understand what *you* say. The child has learned to locate and listen to sounds. She has come to recognize what various tones of voice mean. She knows that the sounds adults make are communication; she has learned to babble and "participate" in these discussions. She has also learned to imitate sounds, first approximately, then with more accuracy. Now, in the Walker stage, she is learning to understand more and more language. And so it continues to be important for you to talk to her as a part of the things you do with her every day. When you are dressing her tell her what you're doing: "Now we'll put on your shirt. Raise your arms so that I can slip it over your head. That's good. See how easily

it goes on that way?" You can also do nursery rhymes together. Pat-a-cake becomes a fun way to encourage imitation as well as to hear the sounds and rhythm of words. As you do these activities, you will see an increase in the child's understanding of single words and phrases. Names of important things, such as "bottle," "mama," "dada," "blanket," "kitty," quickly become part of the child's vocabulary because they are associated with the objects, events, and people that are essential to her life.

Children begin talking in different ways. Most learn to speak gradually, by babbling, imitating, and finally picking up a few words here and there. As mentioned earlier, there are some children who, for one reason or another, appear to show little interest in babbling or speaking and then suddenly start talking, as if they had been saving it up for the right time.

Children need opportunities to use words. For example, you may have learned that when your child goes to the refrigerator she wants her bottle. Going to the refrigerator is her way of telling you to get her something to drink. Instead of immediately getting it for her, encourage her to use language. You might say to her, "What do you want, Stacey?" If she doesn't respond, you can say, "Do you want your bottle?" If she simply nods, say, "Can you say bottle?" If she doesn't respond, repeat the word "bottle" a few times. Chances are, her imitation will be just a sound, or perhaps the first syllable, "ba," but by encouraging her to link sounds to what she wants, you are laying the groundwork for her use of speech to communicate.

When the child was younger, we encouraged you to respond to her sounds by imitating them. In essence we were suggesting that you use "baby talk" and nonsense syllables. This kind of response is important; the high-pitched and generally slower speech which is characteristic of baby talk is helpful to the infant in learning to differentiate sounds. You can continue this kind of talk, but the child also needs to hear real words associated with real events and things. Think about the sounds and language the child hears during the day. Do people speak to her? Do they ask her questions, encourage her to participate, and respond to her attempts to say something? Do they speak to her affirmatively, giving her praise and support while keeping negatives to a minimum?

Children appreciate being talked to about their actions. They love to know you're paying attention to what they're doing. By talking with them about what you see them do, you give them attention as well as link words with their actions: "You just walked all the way around the room!" "Oops,

Types of Speech

Your child needs to hear a diversity of speech. Some of it he'll understand, and some he won't. You don't need to edit your speech to make it comprehensible to him; his language development will be aided more by hearing the things you naturally say than by hearing words and sentences specially made for infants.

You can give your child *information* about what is going on in his environment, or what you're doing. "It's cold outside today." "I'm going to stop in here first." You can name things for your child: "Here are your mittens. Can you say mittens?" "See the dog?" You can give your child *reasons;* even though he won't understand them, he can begin to connect what you do with what you're saying: "I'm going to put these eggs in the pan so they'll cook." *Descriptions* help to expand the child's understanding of different objects, particularly as they relate to one another: "That's a big dog. She's big, brown, and scruffy. She's as big as you are." "How big are you? —sooo big!" *Praise* is important for the child, not only a pat on the back or a hug, but verbal praise as well: "You walked over here all by yourself; that's wonderful." "Look at the terrific tower you made." *Questions* to which you don't expect a verbal answer are a good way to make the child feel he's participating in conversation even when it's difficult for him: "What did you do with your ball? Let's look for it." "Do you know where Maria is? She said she'd be here soon."

down you go." "There, you're up again." "You're really walking a lot today."

Verbal imitation gives the child a chance to try out language and hear the results. You can imitate the child's attempts at speech, and more important, you can ask the child to imitate your speech: "Dog, can you say dog?" After imitating a child's speech, you can elaborate on it. "Blanky; that's right, here's your blanket." This gives the child a chance not only to hear the name of something but to hear it in a sentence.

Many adults have no problem talking to a child, but forget to give the child a chance to talk back. It's important to encourage participation and comments from the child: "What did you do?" "Can you point to what you want?" "That's a block, can you say block?" "That was a nice sound, can you make that sound again?"

When something is about to happen, either something regular such as mealtime, or something out of the ordinary such as a trip to the zoo, talk about it so the child can distinguish certain words that are linked to the event: "Well, it's almost time to eat." "We're going to have to go and cook dinner now. You can bring your toy if you want." "You and I are going on a walk today. Look outside, isn't it a sunny day? Let's see how warm it is out. Oh, it's too cold. We'll have to get our jackets."

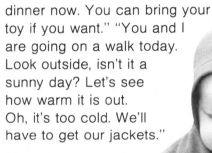

From the child's point of view, the pebbles, sidewalk, leaves, or grass can be just as interesting as a caged lion. Pay attention to what he is interested in exploring so that you can provide him with the words for those things as well as for the things that are probably more interesting to you.

In addition to everyday conversation, children at this stage love to hear stories, and will often "read" a story back to you, imitating the way you hold a book and turn pages, and babbling or saying a word or two in response to a picture. Songs and nursery rhymes are also enjoyable and give the child a chance to make sounds or put in the words she knows. Often a child will spend a long time listening to a record and trying to sing along. Games that use her name are favorites: "Where's Natasha? There's Natasha. Natasha is on the couch." "Whose ball is this? It's Natasha's."

Responding to Needs & Demands

Knowing that he can get a rise out of you with his actions, your child may protest loudly against something he doesn't want to do. He may show off; he may test out a whole range of expressions of anger and affection, waiting to see what you will do. You'll be called on repeatedly to respond to his expressions, both positive and negative, in ways that support his growing sense of self but do not support any kind of disruptive behavior. He needs to know that there are times when *he* can have his way, as well as times when *you* have the final word.

Trying to respond to the child's needs and demands is a difficult and often thankless task. Frequently there are other pressures as well, either in the home or from a job outside the home. In order not to feel overwhelmed, there are several things you can do. First, you need to figure out what your own needs are, and then you need to figure out how to take some time for yourself, even if it's just an hour away from the house, doing something you want to do. Build some time for yourself into your weekly routine.

Second, try to anticipate what the child will do and how you are going to handle the situation when it comes up. It's a good idea to figure out some techniques for dealing with difficult situations before they arise. How can you predict these difficult situations? By the time the child is in the Walker stage you have already had some experience with *no* and the child's striving for independence. This will continue. Think of the times when the child has already challenged you—at feeding time, at naptime, when you want to go somewhere and he doesn't. You have to decide what you are going to allow the child to do in each of these situations and what your limits are.

Third, this is an excellent time to talk with other parents about how they are handling their child at this stage. How much "learning" do they allow at feeding time? How do they get their child to go to bed without a struggle? Parents who are experiencing similar things can provide moral support to each other.

There will be many times when you simply have no patience to deal with the situation. If you explode and handle a situation badly now and then, all is not lost. But if you are aware of what is happening, you can try to anticipate your breaking point and deal with

the situation early, so that it isn't overwhelming for you or the child. Keep in mind that there are no "right answers" to specific questions of childrearing; there are only a range of strategies . . . strategies that can support the child's development.

Relationships and Sense of Self
Consistency builds security

While there are many positive ways in which the child gains a stronger sense of herself—by using and controlling objects, participating in games, helping herself—the negative ways (saying no, being stubborn) are easier for you to see and harder for you to deal with. Saying no and being stubborn are indications that the child is aware of her separateness and is beginning to find ways to assert her will—to say, "I belong to no one but me." Often a child at the Walker stage will begin to fight diaper changes. She may protest loudly at being put down for a nap. If you've established a regular routine and have been consistent in your expectations, this behavior will be easier to deal with. Your child should not get the idea that by being persistent she can always get her way. You can encourage her to

The best support for the child in her relationship with other people is consistency.

include *yes* in her repertoire by playing a choice game: "Do you want the ball?" "No." "Do you want the truck?" "No." "Do you want the doll?" "No." "Do you want the blocks?" "Yes!" Then you give her the blocks. She can also test out the word *no* in the context of games, such as a dropping game in which you and the child each hold an object up in the air and you say, "No, no, no . . . yes!" and both of you drop your objects when you say yes. Eventually the child can be the one to call the shots.

Your child's ability to express herself develops in leaps and bounds in the Walker stage. She grows more sure of herself and is eager to show off the skills she is learning. Strangers become less threatening and can offer a good opportunity for her to try out her new skills and see how others react to them.

Many children enjoy roughhousing and bouncing games, once they are more secure in their mobility and less worried about falling. But it's important not to get carried away and be *too* rough. Often a child will ask for more, even when she's had enough, because she hasn't yet learned to judge such things for herself. So you need to watch for nonverbal messages: her tone of voice, the expression on her face.

Children in the Walker stage may also appear shy at times. They can often be brought out of their shyness gradually through games and activities that you offer. They'll be even more interested if you are willing to play the games with them.

Shyness, however, needn't always be something to overcome. It may lead to very fruitful solitary play, in which the child learns to use her own resources—her emerging intellect and imagination. When the child is playing alone, she needs to know that you are nearby. She may call out to you or glance up from her play just to check where you are and to know that you're there if she needs you. She may suddenly stop playing and follow you around for a few minutes, then return to where she left off in her play. This is an important re-fueling for the child and should be treated as a welcome event: "You're back! Do you want to sit up here with me for a while?" If the child is sure she's welcome, she probably won't stay around very long; she'll want to return to her own activities and explorations.

Whether you are on the lenient or the strict side, if your behavior is consistent, the child will develop a sense of security. She needs to know what is expected of her and what she can expect of you. Of course, it's hard to be responsive to a demanding child day in and day out without struggles, mistakes, and loss of temper. But the child can adjust to a certain amount of adult "unfairness" so long as she knows the lay of the land. If you don't want your child getting into your purse, you should be consistent in telling her not to do it. Even better, you should keep it out of reach. If the child gets the idea that some days she can "break" the rules, either by wheedling you or because you don't seem to care, she'll become confused. She may learn that by pushing she'll get what she wants; then she may push even when there's no point to it.

The child is beginning to realize how powerful she can be in a situation. She can turn on her charm or can throw a terrific temper tantrum. She is learning to use her emotions to get what she wants.

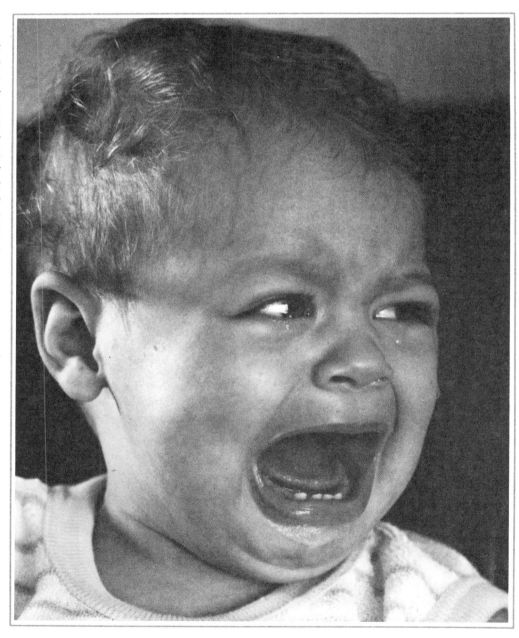

During the Walker stage the child is beginning to make choices. These choices should be ones that the child has the capacity to make. Whether she eats a banana or an apple is a reasonable choice; whether she eats or not, is not. Whether she sleeps with her teddy or with her doll is a reasonable choice; whether she stays up or goes to bed is not. A child is not always aware of whether she is tired, for example, so asking her if she wants to go to bed or stay up is not a good idea. If she is acting tired but fighting you, one of the best strategies is to divert her attention without changing your goal of getting her to bed *now*. Give her a choice, such as which book to read before she goes to sleep or whether she wants to walk or have a piggyback ride to her bedroom. While the idea of choosing is new to the child, she will catch on, and this "technique" will become more and more effective.

Another issue to consider and reconsider as the child grows is how much to do *for* a child, how much to do *with* a child, and what is acceptable to do *to* a child. How much you do for the child is determined by how much help the child asks for, how much she really seems to need, and how able you are to help at a given moment. Often, adults put their own standard on a child's work, and try to push her to make a "better" product. Since this doesn't teach the child much more than the notion that what she did wasn't good enough, this kind of "help" is rarely beneficial. Conversely, some children ask you to help them do things that they could easily do themselves. Such a child is probably asking for attention; it's a good idea to encourage greater self-sufficiency in the child, but it's equally important to make sure that the child is getting attention in other ways.

Once a child is old enough to keep herself occupied with games, many adults fall into the habit of merely "keeping an eye" on the child while they go about their own work. This may be necessary to a certain extent, but it is important to remember that children need to do things *with you*. They can be included in many of your activities: by being held, by being allowed to hold a safe tool or utensil, by being included in conversations.

Through your relationship with your child, you are providing her with the support she needs to develop her sense of self. You are giving her the language she needs to gain a better understanding of people and things. You are providing her with an environment that gives her the physical and emotional support she needs to take those first steps into the world. Although the first signs of independence—self-assertion, solitary play, walking—may be a little scary for both of you, they show that your child is continuing to grow.

Things to Do

Learning How to Make Things Work

Place a favorite toy inside a coffee can or plastic container. Cover the container with a clear plastic lid that has a hole in it large enough for the child's hand to go through, but too small for the toy to come through. The child will have to discover that the lid has to come off to get the object. Encourage her to get the lid off herself.

Giving Names to Things

Encourage your child to name objects by putting a variety of things in a box and going through it with her. Say to the child, "What's in the box? Let's see. It's a . . ." and pause to see if the child says the word before you do.

Those First Steps

When your child begins to show an interest in taking those first steps without holding on, encourage her. Kneel a few feet away from her, stretch out your arms, encouraging her to come to you. When she gets there sweep her up in your arms and set her down facing where she came from—which can be another person or a couch. Encourage her to go back. The first time you try this you should be two or three steps away. If you are too far, she won't risk letting go, even though the distance may seem small to you. As she becomes adept at her new skill, you can gradually increase the distance between you. Challenge her, but be sure she can be successful. Failing over and over again only teaches the child to stop trying.

Learning by Doing

Provide the child with such things as
cups, spoons, plastic bowls, margarine
containers, a wire whisk. Put these items
in a basin of water. She can then "cook"
a meal, imitating your actions of pouring and
stirring. She can pursue this activity on her own,
or you can work with her, giving her words for her actions.
If the weather permits, this is a great activity for the out-of-doors.

Search and Discover

Play a game of hide-and-seek with your child, using some of her toys.
Put the toy in a can so that she cannot see it. The child will probably go
directly to the can and retrieve the toy. After she has mastered this activity,
make it a little more complicated. While she is watching, put the toy in a
can, then take it out and put it in a box. The child will probably look in the
can first, then go to the box. She will follow the order you did. If she finds
the toy, put it in three places before leaving it—from a can to a box to
behind a pillow. If the child has watched you do this, she will repeat your
actions. If she hasn't been watching she will stop searching at the last
place she saw the toy. Play this game with different toys and different
hiding places. See how long she will remain interested in searching.

Exploring the Out-of-Doors

When going for a walk with your child, you will probably be headed
somewhere—whether it be to a park, or the store or simply around the
block. From the child's point of view however, the pebbles, caterpillars,
leaves, or grass along the way can be just as interesting as the swing set
you may be heading for. So give yourself enough time on your walk to
explore. Pay attention to what your child is interested in, providing words
for the things she is discovering.

Building Up/Knocking Down

Make a block tower, or stack empty containers that have lids on them.
Encourage your child to make one like yours. Begin with three blocks. Add
one, then have your child add the next one. See how high a tower you two
can make in this way. (It will soon topple.) Begin again. A variation on this
game is when you build the tower and your child knocks it down.

Chapter VII

With each passing week, your child (now a toddler) learns **The** to *do* a little more—to feed herself, to play on her own, to remember where favorite objects are kept and go after **Doer** them: all the things you've been used to doing for her. She learns to hold and drink from a cup, dress and undress herself (to a certain extent), do simple jobs, clean up messes. She begins to see that objects and activities have a place and order, and she can be very insistent that routines be respected. This is a good time for her to get used to picking up after play. She can also learn to do quite a few self-care tasks—such as combing her hair or washing her face—that others have had to do for her until now. And she'll also delight in running simple errands to please you.

It may be a relief to you that she's more independent, but it's important for you to remain an active supporter. Consider: *Your child has pulled her blocks off the shelf and is building towers with them, then knocking them down. So far, this activity has kept her occupied for ten minutes, and from the looks of things, it could keep her busy for several more.* What is your role in this activity? Obviously, the child doesn't need you to help her build and knock down towers; that she can do well enough on her own. But she does need you in some very crucial ways. For one thing, she needs conversation; you can talk with her about what she's doing. She may ask you to name objects by pointing and saying, "That!" or "What's that?" She may just wave a block and make a "buh" sound. You can support her by saying, "Block, yes, that's a block."

One thing that is characteristic of many children at this stage is an insistence on having things done exactly as they wish them to be done. This is a continuation of the child's earlier attempts to assert her will. She wants to be independent; but the next minute she may give up that independence, wanting to be held and cuddled and wanting your admiration and support for the things she is doing.

One way to handle the situation is to give her a choice: "Do you want to put this shoe on, or do you want me to put it on for you?" One of the characteristics of the Doer is that she wants to do more than she actually can. If she knows how to do something, she wants to do it herself or have you do it *that* way, not some unfamiliar way. She is now able to picture or predict in her mind what is going to happen. When she can create what she has pictured, she has a sense of accomplishment and of control over her environment.

While your child cannot design a game to play with you, she greatly appreciates you picking up on what she is doing and making a game out of it.

The child in the Doer stage is clearly learning new skills, and some of the experimenting and testing that accompany this skill development will challenge your patience.

Since the Doer wants to do everything for herself, she tends to be a messmaker. She can feed herself, but ends up feeding the floor as well. She can take her own toys down from a shelf, but she's not always aware that she has taken everything else off the shelf to get to the toys. Because of the child's messmaking ability, you may be more comfortable feeding her in the kitchen where the mess is easier to clean up, or having her play in a special enclosed playroom. If for your own sanity you feel you need to limit your child this way, make sure you don't isolate her; she needs to be around people and included in activities. If she's had her dinner earlier in the kitchen, give her a cracker or piece of fruit to eat as she sits with the rest of the family during their dinner.

The best way to support the child's learning is to take advantage of naturally occurring situations. Your toddler will be around when you are cooking meals, so let her help stir the pancake batter for breakfast and then hold the plate while you serve the pancakes. These activities help the child learn how to use household objects; they also teach her about how things are done in our culture. These times with you will help her grow and learn every bit as much as playing games with her or doing specially designed activities.

Physical Abilities
Controlling actions, refining skills

The Doer is learning to control her actions—to run, jump, hop, kick, throw a ball, even do somersaults and walk backwards. Her interest in what's going on in the household gives her opportunities to refine her skills. She learns to open and close a variety of containers (so make sure dangerous bottles,

Toilet Training

Toilet training can easily become a battleground; it can become the focal point in your child's struggles for independence. He may see that saying no when you suggest using the toilet is a good way to get you angry. If that is the case, it's best not to force the issue. If you dig in your heels and insist, the child is likely to do the same, and both of you will be left with bad feelings about the whole experience. It's best if you can be flexible! If the child is open to using the toilet, then go ahead. On the days he refuses, follow his lead and be patient. Remember that toilet training is not as obvious a necessity to your child as it is to you. When he's able to provide you with cues as to when he needs to use the toilet, take him up on them. He may also learn that he can use these cues when he doesn't really need to go; he is then likely to eliminate the minute you have him rediapered. The process does indeed take patience. But be assured: your child *will* eventually get tired of being in diapers and learn to use the toilet.

medicines, cleaning fluids, etc. are out of reach), to build and knock down block towers, to remove the wrapping from packages or unroll the toilet paper, to make scribbles and dots on paper in imitation of writing, and to carry several objects at once. She is also able to recognize and say when she's hungry or thirsty or getting tired (although she's unlikely to go voluntarily to bed).

When she needs to urinate or defecate she is aware of it now. In addition, she has some control of the muscles involved; she may be ready to begin toilet training. By now you are probably aware of her body posture when she's eliminating. When you

see the signs, you can take her to the toilet and put her on it, making her aware that when she needs to eliminate she can let you know and can begin to use the toilet.

Understanding the World
Making things happen

Your child's understanding of the world continues to develop dramatically in the Doer stage. She learns that barking means there's a dog nearby, that putting on a coat is a signal someone is leaving the house, that a picture "stands for" something real. She also learns to recognize an object from a variety of clues (how it smells, how it feels, how it tastes, what it sounds like). When she sees only part of an object, she understands that the rest of it is there. You can make this new understanding a part of the games you play with her: show her a part of a familiar object to see if she can figure out what's missing; when a dog barks and she hears, say "Where's the doggy?" or "What was that?"

It's fascinating to see with what vigor Doers go about the tasks they see as important; their energy for their work suggests that there is some natural, intrinsic motivation in learning, and that a good learning environment can be any setting that offers the child an opportunity to safely explore and participate in events—any situation that supports her activities. A child's play can take as many forms as there are children; it all depends on the materials at hand and the encouragement given.

What games does your child invent for herself? Does she like to pile boxes and knock them over? Does she pick up a rag when you are cleaning and help you dust? Perhaps she sings songs to herself, or plays peek-a-boo in the mirror.

What kind of objects or toys does your child respond to most? Does she like small things that require careful coordination to grasp, such as popcorn? Does she particularly enjoy objects that make a noise? Does she play make-believe games with stuffed animals? The toys and games your child already likes will give you ideas about what else she might like, and what she is learning at the moment. She learns through her observations and testing of ideas. The more she is able to test and observe, the broader her understanding will be.

The Doer is fascinated with mechanical toys and can learn to work them herself. She is challenged and entranced by toys that require her to solve problems (such as stacking rings, piling blocks, emptying and

filling containers). She will struggle to master difficulties, both physical (such as holding a pencil so that it makes a proper mark) and intellectual (such as fitting shapes into holes). Her earlier attitude of "What happens if . . . ?" has given way to a new attitude: "How can I make this happen?"

The Doer understands that objects exist even when she can't see them. She can remember that her dumptruck and sand toys are in the sandbox. You can now ask her to recall where she left things, and to go get them herself. She's also grasped the difficult idea that an object can be moved from place to place and still exist. You can see this as you play hide-and-seek games with her. Hide a toy in a box and move the box to another part of the room; she knows the toy is still in the box, no matter where you put the box. And she's no longer as fearful that when you leave the room you've vanished; she understands that although you are not visible, you still exist.

Now that she can think about objects, in the sense that she has a mental picture of them, she begins to see that there are similarities between objects, that some go together with others. She's able to look at sets of objects and begins to understand the concept of a "collection." She begins to understand the idea of matching one to one—one for me, one for you; one block in this can and one block in that can. Sorting activities encourage her to notice the ways things are alike and the ways they're different.

Overall, the Doer's world is becoming more predictable. She knows in advance, for example, that when she puts a string of beads into a tall wobbly tube, the tube will be knocked over, so she holds on to the tube or adjusts her actions in some way to make sure it doesn't tip over.

Sharing

It's difficult for children at this stage to actually *play* together with the give and take the term usually implies. However, they do play next to each other, and they may speak to each other, hand each other toys, and show affection with pats and kisses in imitation of their parents. But, in general, "me" and "mine" dominate the child's approach to play. Very little sharing occurs. Learning to share comes much later when the child is able to understand someone else's point of view, and when he can begin to see some payoffs for himself (for instance, he gets something else he wants if he shares). Asking him to share at the Doer stage would be asking him to give up a part of himself, with no assurance that he will get it back; that's the way he understands what you want him to do.

He will also have difficulty sharing *you,* especially when he's tired, when other children arrive on the scene, or when you are out together in public. At these times, your child will need to know that you are there for him. He may even punch or slap "intruders" or cling tightly to you in fear, jealous of the attention you show to others. There will be times when you are talking with someone else and don't want to be interrupted. If your toddler is constantly pulling at you to pay attention to him, give him something to play with while you're busy. Allow him to

be nearby even though you're not doing something with him. Occasionally you can glance in his direction and give a reassuring nod and smile. If he goes to another room he may need to come back and "interrupt" more than once. Let him know you are still busy, that you and he can do something later. This lets him know he isn't forgotten; it also lets him know that he has to share you with others.

Communication
The power of speech

Being with a child who is learning to talk is exciting. When the child comes up with a fairly recognizable name for something, both you and she are pleased. As language skill develops, there is a new level at which you and the child can communicate.

In our culture, great emphasis is placed on people's ability to use the language well. Adults get great pleasure and satisfaction when they are able to put a thought or feeling into words. When a child says "bottle" she's not, of course, communicating deep thoughts and heavy concepts; she's simply giving a name to an object. Yet you'll find yourself sitting up and taking notice when it happens.

As your child begins to understand the power of her speech, she'll want to increase her vocabulary. She'll want you to name objects for her. (But don't always supply the names of things before she has a chance to try to name them herself.) You can question her and get her to respond with words. You can repeat her attempts and encourage her to imitate you. You can demonstrate to her that when she asks for something in words, she gets a response from you. Explanations are good because they give the child a sense of belonging, but long-winded "grown-up" explanations ("I didn't get enough sleep last night, and since I have to go to a meeting later this afternoon, I need a nap") can be frustrating if the adult expects something, such as quiet. The child will learn to tune out a constant stream of words if she can't connect them with what you're doing or if the words are too complex. On the other hand, words associated with actions will enrich the child's understanding of the language and eventually lead to the use of new words.

The number of words the child can understand is increasing rapidly. Your toddler can follow simple directions, point to named objects and body parts, understand simple stories. Her own name is likely to become a favorite, and she'll begin referring to herself by name: "Jennie go."

She is developing a small vocabulary of key words, such as "up," "bye-bye," "pretty," which she combines with names of things to communicate ideas: "Up, mommy" can mean "I want you to pick me up, mommy." "All gone" may signify "I've eaten all my food." You can use your toddler's battery of key words and phrases when speaking with her and giving explanations. And you can elaborate on her two-word sentences; your response to "Daddy go" might be, "That's right, daddy is going shopping now."

Your child will get a great sense of mastery and satisfaction when you listen and respond to her language.

As you talk with your child she may repeat the last word you said, as if trying to get the feeling of the sentence. You can support her efforts by praising her and repeating the word. Often she'll speak in order to get a response from you rather than communicate a thought. So even if you have difficulty understanding what she means, always acknowledge her efforts. She'll talk as she plays, carrying on conversations with dolls and animals. She'll imitate animal sounds. She'll hum or sing to herself. She may enjoy "talking on the phone," perhaps using a block for a phone and pretending you are on the other end of the line.

This is a time for active encouragement of language learning. One way to do this is to begin to develop in your child an interest in reading, by making books a part of her everyday life. Even though she can't learn to read at this point, she can get used to handling books, turning pages, and enjoying the pictures. Sturdy, heavy-duty cloth or plastic books will stand up best against curious fingers. She'll also learn that she can find out new things from books, and that books have fascinating stories inside them. Introduce books when you and your child can sit down together and not be interrupted. At first the child may be interested in a book for only a few minutes, but she'll soon be interested for much longer periods of time, especially if reading together becomes a regular part of your relationship, a bond between you.

While those first books may have only one picture on a page and represent only one type of object—animals, foods, household items—your child will soon be interested in books in which there's more than one object on a page or some more complex action is shown. Beyond that, the child's interest will expand to include colorful books which have imaginary as well as real objects. Books are an excellent way for the child to learn more about her world and to increase her vocabulary. Many conversations can take place between you and your child as you read books together.

Role Play

The Doer loves to mimic the actions of others. At first he may copy you without really understanding what the action means. As he tries out various actions he learns more about what they mean. This is the beginning of role play.

Role play is a way for children to express their understanding of what happens around them. They use it to try out new behavior and to repeat both pleasurable and difficult experiences. They use it to re-create their world and to re-examine parts of it. When a young child is playing with a doll, feeding and cuddling it, role play is occurring. Role play gives your child a chance to re-live events, but with more control and from his own point of view.

Your child's role play reflects the messages he's receiving about how things are done. He may wash and comb his doll's hair the way he's seen his mother do her own. He may also imitate behavior he picked up outside the home—from neighbors, relatives, TV, and other toddlers. Some of this behavior you may approve of and some, such as banging a doll around, may make you concerned about what your child is feeling and why. Since the child is acting out his perceptions of behavior and not necessarily being "bad," it's not as important to correct him as it is to provide him with other examples, and to be aware of what he may be observing.

Even at this early age your child will be sensitive to the messages you and society are giving him about the roles of men and women. No matter how concerned you are about sex-role stereotyping, it's what actually happens each day in the child's world that he takes in and makes his own. Does he see men and women doing the same or different tasks? The greater the variety of behavior he has a chance to observe (and re-enact in role play), the more options he'll feel he has as he grows.

Many people are finding that the traditional distinctions between male and female roles are less and less suited to the demands of today's society. As a result, many parents are consciously choosing to expand the kinds of experiences their children have. Instead of raising their daughter to be a "little lady" and their son to be a "little gentleman," they focus on trying to help their child, of either sex, be an inquisitive, active, emotionally secure, caring individual. You will need to examine your beliefs carefully; as your child begins to role play the multiplicity of actions and situations he's already witnessed, it will be up to you to guide him in the directions you value most.

Supporting Your Child's Play

At times, your child may be able to get his toys out and start to play with them, but he may lose direction and idly push them here and there. To help him out, you can get down on the floor and play alongside him. If, for example, he's playing with some blocks fairly listlessly, you might take three of them to build a tower. Watch what he does. Does he follow your lead? He may want to be invited to join in: "I just built a tower. Do you want to build a tower?" Or he may want to play a game with you, such as knocking your tower down. He might enjoy taking turns—first he adds a block to the tower, then you add one. You might offer him some toys to place on his tower, or blocks of different sizes, or a box to serve as a steady base. You can also contribute to your child's activities by imitating him. You might, for example, sit down beside him and build a tower like the one he's building. This says to your child that what he's doing is worthy of attention. It also helps him to think about what he is doing—that is, to compare it with what *you* are doing.

Relationships and Sense of Self
"I can do it myself"

While the child is becoming more aware of others and their needs, she is also becoming more adamant about asserting her own will. She is continually shifting between doing things on her own and seeking to be reassured that you are still there for her when she needs you. Through mastery of tasks and locomotion, the child's sense of herself has become intense. She is learning that she can say no, make choices, protest decisions, cooperate or not cooperate. This gives her a sense of autonomy, an attitude of "I can do it myself."

She will give orders to others and resent being made to do something; she will press for something she wants and resist pressure from others. Many children who earlier were even-tempered become whiny or even stormy at this stage, throwing tantrums with little provocation. Tantrums may be an indication of the child's ambivalence about being independent.

The Doer seems to need to reject all that is familiar and known in an attempt to define who she is for herself. You may find yourself ready to tear your hair out with the changing moods. And because nothing seems to work all the time you are likely to feel very inadequate at meeting the emotional needs of your young child.

It is important for you, in responding to your child's tantrums, not to get caught up in the struggle of the moment. Let the child feel the constancy of your love, despite the fact that you may not like her behavior at the moment.

Your child will demand that schedules remain the same. She will want routines to be consistent so that her world is predictable and she has some control over what happens. If she is expected to eat in her chair *sometimes,* and at other times is fed while sitting on the kitchen floor, and at still other times is expected to help herself from a table set up in the yard, she will feel confused. If on some days you insist she bed down for a

During the Doer stage the child becomes more sociable.

nap and on other days you give in to her whining and let her skip the nap, it will be difficult for her to feel that her world is consistent and thus coherent.

The child's goals are becoming more complicated. While earlier she was engrossed in tasks like learning to walk, now her goals are more socially oriented and complex. She may try, for example, not only to walk, but to keep up with siblings in a game, or to walk along with you. This requires much greater coordination of her actions and fitting those actions to someone else's pace and style.

In the household the child can use more objects. She can use a spoon (in her own way, of course), undress herself (even when you don't want her to), and help in simple household tasks. She is learning to do more than simply use the objects; she is learning to use them for specific purposes. To a certain extent, these purposes are determined by others. The child is realizing that she is part of a larger world. Though she is still very "egocentric," her recognition of how she fits into things has begun to shift. Before, she assumed that she was the center of the universe and everything existed for her interest, support, use, and gratification. Now she is beginning to see that others have needs and feelings and that she has to differentiate between what belongs to others (including feelings) and what belongs to her.

The child's increasing competence gives her a greater sense of security with regard to other people. Her interest in the actions of others makes her much more sociable. Her interactions with people are becoming longer and more varied. She enjoys playing games, sharing tasks around the house, teasing playfully, and exchanging signs of affection. She may want to play with you for as much as half an hour at a time. She takes an increased interest in watching and imitating both adults and other children.

Your child will try out the word *no* in a variety of situations in an attempt to assert her power. Frequently she'll be genuinely surprised if you take her seriously. On the other hand, there will be times when she really means it. *No* is an indication of the beginning of decision-making. The child is beginning to realize that she can make choices. She refuses to eat foods today that were her favorites yesterday. She refuses to take that bath that was once so enjoyable (although once she gets in she's likely to experience the fun of

Coping With Your Toddler's Shifting Moods

The Doer stage is full of unpredictable behavior. You may feel you have no control as your child struggles to assert himself while making constant demands on you. But there are, of course, many things you can do.

First, maintain a calm, low-key but loving attitude. Yelling back at your child or cajoling will probably cause further confusion and upset. He is looking for consistency and support. If you are inconsistent he'll learn to push harder.

Second, keep on top of situations by considering them from the child's point of view. Have you given him a choice or is he being backed into a corner? Is he included in what's going on? Does he have something interesting to occupy his attention? (When cleaning, give him a toy broom or rag to use alongside you. When you have visitors, help him choose toys that he can play with in the same room without requiring your attention.)

Third, maintain a regular routine and give him choices within that routine. For example, do *not* let a child protest his way out of going grocery shopping with you, but *do* give him a choice of whether or not to bring along a favorite toy.

Fourth, watch your child carefully for signs of whether he wants support or independence. Often he won't know, and he will get fussy, especially if he's tired. Try to help him find a balance. Offer to cuddle him frequently, so that he can refuse cuddling and choose his own activity without being afraid he won't have a chance to be cuddled again soon.

Finally, in disciplining your child, remember only to make "threats" that you can and will carry out. If your child refuses to wear his hat in cold weather, a reasonable threat might be, "You will have to come inside if you don't keep your hat on." An unreasonable threat would be, "You'll never go outside again if you don't keep your hat on." Lifting the child bodily into bed if he refuses to go on his own may be necessary at times, but spanking the child makes no sense to him; he won't understand why he's being punished. Try to think of responses that enforce the routines without being a punishment. After all, the message you want to give is, "This is the rule," not, "You are bad." The toddler's time frame is short, so telling him he'd better stop or daddy will punish him when he gets home will not have the meaning you want it to have for him: if daddy arrives and he rushes to greet him and daddy spanks him for something he did hours before, he learns only to fear daddy.

waterplay as before). At the same time, she'll also be retreating periodically into self-comforting behavior—finding her favorite blanket and lying down with it awhile, sucking her thumb, climbing up on the couch where she can be close to you, sure that you are still there for her through all her negativity.

The child seems to be on a swing that is going higher and higher. She is reaching further and further toward independence. . . and the swings back to dependence are proportionately greater. On some days she may want to return to eating baby foods, and although she is adept at self-feeding, she may refuse to eat unless you feed her; on other days she'll want to feed herself and will reject all offers of help.

On one level she wants to take control; on another she needs you to let her know that you are in control. The child, in short, is ambivalent. She'll be angry when she can't have her way, but if she gets her way all the time she becomes frightened because she's not really capable of taking full control. Therefore, in supporting the child at the Doer stage, it's important to continue to maintain firm limits. The child will need reassurance that you are actually in control even though there are some things *she* can control. More than ever before you will need to be clear about what you expect of the child at feeding times, during her play, when people are visiting or when you're busy, when it's time to clean up or go to bed, when it's bathtime or when there are jobs or tasks to do.

Help the child feel secure each step of the way. For example, if you are taking her with you on a trip to visit friends, explain to her, slowly and carefully, where you are going and for how long. She may not understand all the words and their meaning, but your inclusion of her in the process will not be lost on her. You can show her pictures of the people you're visiting, if she knows them, and encourage her to learn their names. Adults often forget that children don't have the patience to sit and do nothing for long periods of time, so help her choose one or two of her favorite toys to take along . . . and help her explain to the toys where you are going. It's not only a good idea to take along toys and other "entertainment," it's also important to help the child focus on activities she can do during the trip.

The Doer stage is one in which accidents can easily happen because the child is able to get into things but isn't aware of the dangers. (The stove should be off limits, whether it's turned on or not.) This is a time when children can easily and innocently wander away from a yard, or open interesting bottles, or move chairs around the room and climb on them to reach high objects. Once again: you will need to establish clear limits and enforce them.

Your child still wants what she wants when she wants it, but she's able, to a limited degree, to understand the concept of "wait" and to accept a substitute for what she wants (a piece of fruit instead of a candy bar, a cannister of beans instead of your favorite necklace). Let her know how you feel when you don't want her to do something; give her reasons, and also let her know that you love her no matter what she does. If you are angry at something she does, let the anger out. Tell her *why* you're angry, and try to let her know that though she did something bad, she's not a bad person.

One way to support the child during this stage is to make her feel included. Inclusion can come in a number of ways. It comes from letting your child sit with other family members during meals. It comes when the child feels there is some choice she can make in a situation; for instance, when dressing the child, you can offer her a choice between two shirts she wants to wear, or you can let her choose which favorite toy to take along on a stroll outdoors. For every limit you place on her ("It's time to go to bed"), it's important to give her some choice in the process

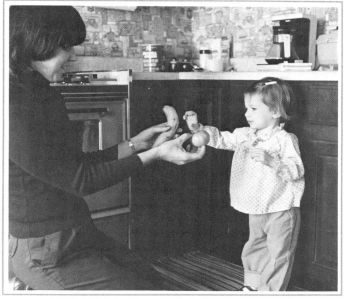

("Which story should we read tonight?"). Bedtime is not an option, but the story to be read is a legitimate choice for the child.

When limits are clear, you and the child know what to expect. You also know when the "rules" have been broken. A threat you don't or can't carry out will just confuse and anger the child. "No more banana if you rub it in your hair" is a realistic threat. "No more food for the rest of the day if you don't stop that" is not a realistic threat. The classic boogey-man threats— "If you're not good the boogey-man will get you"—only frighten the child; eventually she sees that you don't mean what you say because the boogey-man never comes. The child needs to see real consequences that are in proportion to the misbehavior.

Your child is coming into her own, yet she needs you. She needs you really to be in control. She needs you to let her do things by herself, yet be there when she falters. She needs you to be consistent despite her swings between independence and dependence. These needs will be even more intense as she enters the Tester stage.

Things to Do

Let's Pretend

One wonderful thing about children at this stage is that they don't have to have the "real" thing in their play. They like to pretend. They are quite content to use a stick for a comb, or a screwdriver to mark the edge of a road; they will use boxes as houses or barns or suitcases, etc. By using things around the house (*and* your imagination), you can help the child create her own story. Give names to objects ("chair" or "bed" or "car") and they become that for the child. "Let's pretend" is a game for both parent and child.

What's Wrong?

Solving problems is a new skill the child is developing at this stage. You can create situations to help her practice this skill. For example, put a few round stacking blocks on a stick and roll it along. Then add a square stacking block. Give the blocks back to the child and see if she can figure out how to make them roll again. If she seems stumped, take them back, remove the square block and repeat the process. Encourage her to watch what you are doing. She will soon discover that the square block keeps the toy from rolling.

Pictures, Pictures, Pictures

At this stage, children enjoy picture books. Animal books are always an early favorite. When introducing a book to the child, go through it with her, identifying the pictures. Once the child is familiar with the pictures, ask her to "find the horse in the book, or the cow, or the goat." Allow her to search through the book to find the correct animal. You can also demonstrate the sound that each animal makes. Then ask her to find "the animal that goes moo." Another book activity is to begin helping your child identify colors: "Find the brown animal." "Where is the blue sky?" Encourage her to "read" the book to you by having her go through it, repeating all that she has learned page by page.

Moving to Music

Do dance exercises together to music. Encourage your child to move her body in a variety of ways—bending, stretching, somersaulting, swaying, balancing.

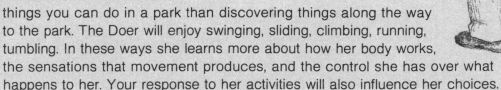

Getting Out and About

Unlike the Walker, the Doer will be more interested in things you can do in a park than discovering things along the way to the park. The Doer will enjoy swinging, sliding, climbing, running, tumbling. In these ways she learns more about how her body works, the sensations that movement produces, and the control she has over what happens to her. Your response to her activities will also influence her choices.

See How It Goes

Show the child how to operate a mechanical toy. Hand it to her and see if she can operate it. If she hands it back to you, show her once again how to operate it. Then give it back to her and let her try. Once she can operate the toy, give her another one, but this time don't show her how it works. Instead, see if she can figure out how it works herself.

Sorting: "Things That Go Together"

Give your child two empty cans and a collection of two different kinds of objects (for example, buttons and small blocks). To encourage the child to begin sorting, place a button in one can and a block in the other. Then hand the child a button and encourage her to put it with the other button. Then give her a block. See if she'll continue to sort the objects.

Later on, when your child has had some practice sorting, challenge her. Don't provide any clues. Suggest to the child that she can sort a group of miscellaneous objects into two boxes. Watch to see what she does as she makes her own choices about putting objects together. Her reasons for sorting them the way she does may not be clear to you. But when obvious groupings are made, you can say, "Oh, I see you put all the red things together." It may well be that one of the boxes contains objects that go together in one way (they all have handles) while the other contains everything else. You can show the child other ways of putting things together, but don't "correct" her; her sorting will make sense in some way!

Chapter VIII

The Tester

Many parents refer to the Tester stage as the "terrible twos." As the name suggests, when the child enters this stage, most parents experience unexpected difficulties. Your child may change quickly and dramatically from moment to moment—from being angelic to throwing tantrums, from demanding your assistance to refusing any kind of help.

The child is "testing" many things; foremost among them is her independence. She wants to do much more than she can actually do on her own, so she is constantly frustrated. She wants to put on her own shoes, fetch her own sweater out of the drawer, feed herself. She may indeed be able to do some of these things, but when it takes her fifteen minutes to put on one shoe, or when most of her breakfast ends up on the floor, your patience as well as her autonomy is being put to the test.

The child is also testing her effect on people and objects and situations. She is curious about how you will react to what she does, and she is testing her ability to make things happen. She learns how to provoke you—stalling before bedtime, dawdling over food. You will inevitably react to her actions calmly on some days and with anger on others. You shouldn't feel guilty about losing your temper; just make it clear to the child that it is not she that displeases you but her behavior.

Because the Tester is searching out your responses to her actions, many otherwise ordinary situations can become battles. While cleaning the carpet you may suddenly find the power cut; you turn around to see your child grinning broadly, holding the power cord. You calmly take it out of her hand, plug it in again, and go back to work. As soon as you turn your back, she yanks it out again. This time you're a little less friendly: "O.K., that's enough, go find something else to play with." The third time she does it you feel your anger rising. Is she trying to make you angry, or is she genuinely exploring, trying to find out what happens when she pulls the cord? The answer is probably that she *is* curious about the power cord, but when she gets a dramatic reaction from you, exploring becomes a provocative game.

Ignoring her may work; it may also lead to frustration and a tantrum. If you get angry and yell at your child, you may stop her temporarily but you're likely to frighten her or make her more stubborn and fussy. If you have the time and patience, you can stop your work and play with her, but she may discover from this that she can get what she wants by interrupting you. When you are angry and frustrated to the point of wanting to slap the child, it may be necessary to put her in another room.

On most occasions you can probably redirect her energy. One way is to include her in what you're doing. You might ask her to come help dust while you sweep. Another strategy is to have her choose which of her toys she's going to play with while you work: "Rachael, I need to clean,now. Your dumptruck is by the couch, and your blocks are on the shelf. Which do you want to play with now while I work?"

Generally, the wisest thing to do with your child as she tests her will and your tolerance is to help her find something she can do, some choice she can make. Explain to her why you are offering her something other than what she wanted to do. Since she wants to have control, it's easy for small events to turn into big ones, leaving you both feeling angry, frustrated, and spiteful. You, in fact, have control—you can always pick her up and remove her from the situation. She cannot do the same with you. But in developing a sense of herself as a competent person, your child needs to feel there are things she can control. By giving her choices, you are responding to this need. At the same time, you are establishing the limits you feel are necessary. Both of you can come out of the situation feeling good. There will be times when she will accept this approach, though at other times she may dissolve in tears. In the latter case, all you can do is accept her tears. They'll pass.

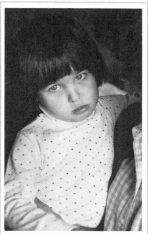

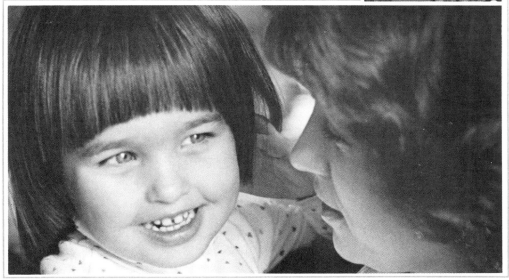

The Tester stage is a time of physical adjustment to the growth spurt of the first two years of life. (It is during this stage that the child reaches half of her adult height.) By now your child is probably able to run, use her hands with enough skill to take things apart, and master combinations of movements—such as standing on a chair to pull down magazines from a shelf. While this control allows her to expand her play activities and her learning, it can also present a challenge to you. She can quickly learn to imitate things she sees you doing, including such "fun" activities as taking the cassette player apart with a screwdriver, or pulling leaves off your favorite plant. She'll be fascinated with her ability to do, yet she won't understand much about safety. The Tester doesn't really understand the idea of destruction. If she takes your plant apart, it's not much different to her from taking a block tower apart, except that one action pleases you and the other does not.

Another testing area is language. Now, more and more, words will accompany what the child is doing. But her words are not always meant to provide you with information; as she goes about her play she'll talk to herself, trying out words and sounds. She is able to express simple concepts with short, almost telegraphic sentences ("Rita go store"). But more often than not, she's just trying things out, testing. She may say words that seem to make no sense or have nothing to do with what is going on around her. She may speak aloud some thoughts about events that have happened earlier, or about dreams. She'll learn the word *why,* and will use it not only to find out reasons but also to keep a conversation going. She'll probably say many things you have trouble understanding; asking her to repeat what she said may not help, especially if it's the meaning, rather than just the words, that's unclear. Let her know you appreciate what she said, even if you had trouble understanding it, and respond with something that expands on her efforts; she'll reward you by continuing to try things out in this highly creative form of testing.

Another creative form of testing takes place in the child's play with objects. The Tester can think about how things work without having to actually go through each step, and a whole new range of ideas begins to develop. How are things alike or different? What happens when you combine objects or take them apart? Now you might see your child pick up an object in her shape box, look at it, look over all the holes, and place the object in the correct hole rather than randomly trying every hole. This shows that she is thinking out some actions in her mind; no longer does she have to try each possibility to see whether or not it works.

The Tester can think before he acts, and does so with increasing frequency. He has a longer attention span and can plan and carry out an activity, such as experimenting with water and containers.

The Tester has a longer attention span, more ability to do what she has set out to do, and more interest in spending time in play sessions with you: taking paint and a bucket of water outside to paint rocks, throwing a ball back and forth, making up a game to play with checkers and a board. She'll be much more interested in playing than in following rules or making attractive things. A good part of the fun at this stage is in the doing; the child is not likely even to be interested in keeping the end product. (A picture is fun to make, but there's no need to explain it to someone or to keep it.)

In order to have a satisfying day, your child will need plenty of active outdoor games. She needs to exercise her body by swinging, running, jumping, climbing, somersaulting, rolling, and dancing. It's especially important to let her get some exercise before a nap or bedtime; otherwise it may be difficult for her to wind down enough to sleep.

Fostering Independence

Dressing

(1) In selecting clothes for your child, keep in mind that clothing with elastic waistbands is easier to manipulate than clothing with zippers and buttons. Shirts that pull over the head are better than those that close in the back.

(2) Have a special place where the child's clothes are stored—*a place that he can reach*. Encourage him to select his own clothes. He may come up with some unfashionable combinations, but if he likes them together, let him wear them. If you're uncomfortable with this, let him choose between two shirts you've picked out that go with the pants he has on.

(3) Have a place where the child can put dirty clothes.

(4) Let him help with the laundry—sorting clothes, folding his clean clothes and placing them where they belong.

Feeding

The child is now able to chew larger pieces of food. You won't have to cut up or strain all his food any longer. He can bite off a piece from a section of apple, he can eat a piece of toast, and so on. There are still some things you'll need to cut, though, such as meat and hot foods that he can't pick up and bite off.

Toilet training

(1) Give the child a word or symbol that he can use when he needs to use the toilet. Some parents like to use grown-up words like "urinate"; others are more comfortable with more common language like "weewee." Use whatever is most comfortable for you.

(2) Put the child on the toilet without diapers on so he can begin to feel what it is like.

(3) When facial expressions and sounds indicate the child is having a bowel movement, put him on the toilet so that he begins to associate the toilet with the act.

(4) If the child seems to have a bowel movement at a fairly predictable time of day, put him on the toilet at about that time. But don't leave him there for more than a few minutes if he doesn't move his bowels.

(5) Follow the child's lead in toilet training. *It cannot be forced.*

You can help your child express his energy by making sure he gets plenty of outdoor (or active indoor) exercise.

Physical Abilities
Coordination and mastery

You might wonder where your child gets all her energy, and what on earth you can do to keep up with her. Your child's body is continuing to develop, and she continues to work to gain control of it. By now she is able to do many things: walk, run, hop, and she seems to learn new skills every day.

Her self-help skills are getting better and better—she can wash her own hands, begin to use the toilet with occasional success, pull off her own clothes at night, and even put some of them back on in the morning. She can learn to use a fork and spoon, and will sometimes want to use that skill; at other times, she may refuse to even touch a spoon, using her hands instead to play with, throw, sort, and occasionally eat her food.

Her body rhythm is changing, which may cause erratic eating: one day she'll eat you out of house and home and then she may go for two or three days showing no interest in food at all. She needn't eat all that you provide at a meal; her body will tell her when she needs food. If there's a choice available when she eats she will choose correctly, giving herself the range of foods that she needs. At meals she recognizes foods and remembers what she likes and doesn't like. Being able to say no to some foods and even ask for others gives her a sense of control over her eating.

Your child's sense of self is bolstered throughout the day, as he shows what he prefers, joins in ongoing activities, and sees his effect on people and events.

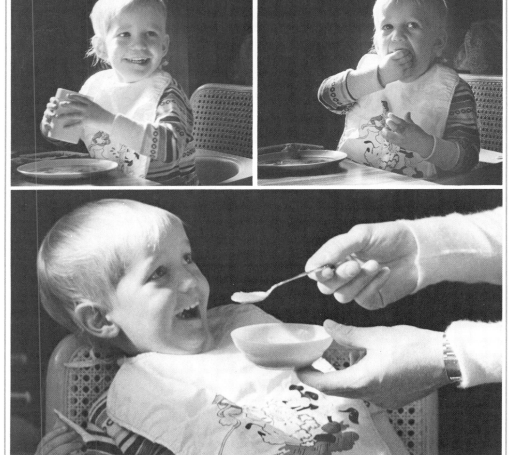

New foods, served along with some favorites, are best introduced when the child is hungry. Beware, though, of fickleness: things that the child has never been able to get enough of will suddenly be spurned and replaced by another set of favorites. While realizing that the child's eating habits may be erratic, you may still be concerned about her getting the variety and quantity she needs. If so, don't hesitate to check with your doctor.

During the Tester stage your child becomes more and more skilled in using her hands. She begins to coordinate complex hand and eye

movements, such as those involved in putting together five-piece puzzles. She learns to insert shapes into a shape box and pegs into a pegboard. The more she can learn to do physically, the more likely she is to understand how things work. Her physical development at this stage is not so much a matter of achieving landmarks as of using and broadening the abilities she already has. Learning to run, climb, and hop teach her more about the physical world than just walking could. All of these skills require physical control and coordination; she is motivated to master them because she knows her mastery will please you and the other people who are important in her life.

Play

As was evident in the Doer stage, "play is the child's work," and you will help your child grow if you take the time to stop and think about what he needs for his play, what kinds of play you can encourage, and what the best conditions are for his play. Play does several things for your child. It helps him develop his physical abilities—the "large muscle" skills as well as the "fine motor" skills. It helps him to sharpen his senses. It gives him opportunities to expand and strengthen his vocabulary. In play he can attend to and persist with a task—in a word, he can *concentrate*.

The Tester will play with all kinds of materials. He'll imitate people and scenes he remembers and will use dolls and toy animals and blocks to stand for characters in his games.

When purchasing toys, look for ones that can be used in many ways. Objects that can be used only one way do not challenge the child's curiosity and creativity. Tinker toys, Legos, and building blocks are invaluable; the child can create many things from them and use them to stand for other objects when role playing.

The materials your child uses in his play need not be store-bought toys. They can be any number of things you might find around the house. The child's imagination will lead the way! An oatmeal box can be a tom-tom, and also a tower, and also a container to drop things into, and also a scoop for sand.

A child's play should allow him to be active. He needs to use his body and his energy. He needs to learn how to judge size and distance, and to recognize shape and texture. He'll learn through his actions. When he's playing with materials—scraps of paper, crayons, tape and scissors, fabrics, beads—he'll be much more interested in the process of playing than in making something. Most adults can't resist asking, "What are you making?" The child doesn't really care, but if he responds, he'll

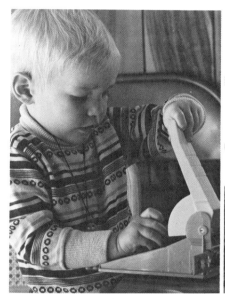 

say what his creation looks like to him at the moment you asked.

Often your role at playtimes will not be starting or teaching the game but responding to and expanding the game. You might suggest new things to try: "We've been rolling the ball, now let's try bouncing it." You might suggest additional objects to use: "Let's go into the kitchen and see if we can find something to use for your monster's house." You can ask questions and help keep conversations going: "I see you put these two blocks together. What are you going to do with this one?" You can try to figure out what he's concentrating on, and encourage him: "You put one hat on this bottle, and one hat on that bottle. Can you find another hat to put on this bottle over here?"

The child will know when older siblings are playing and will want to be included (or better, be the center of things). He is not yet able to play with other children in a give-and-take way, but he'll probably enjoy playing alongside others who are as busy as he. Unfortunately, though, his good will is likely to be short-lived; since he is unable to see things from another's point of view and is so possessive, squabbles will quickly arise.

Many play situations teach your child what it means to wait. For example, when playing a board game with his siblings, a child at the beginning of the Tester stage might pick up his marker and hit the board with it—in imitation of the others—whenever he feels like it. But as he gets older, he'll learn to wait his turn, or at least respond to a signal from others. He won't be concerned with rules, of course, but he will listen to the directives of his older brothers and sisters.

Sense of Self
Becoming the best she can be

The Tester sees herself as a person who can do things, and often she's not very patient with having you do things for her. But this is a shaky time for your child. Sometimes she will be brave and try things that are more difficult than she can handle (for example, climbing to the top of a jungle gym, then finding she can't get down). At other times, she won't even try to do things she did with no trouble yesterday.

During the times of self-confidence, the Tester can be an utter delight. Many parents find that for the first time they can relax and really enjoy their child's antics. They feel more comfortable communicating with their child because she's beginning to use language and gestures that are more familiar to them—more like what adults use.

She is developing a sense of humor. She has learned that there are ways she can mimic others that will bring laughter from the household. She can scowl the way you do, repeat television commercials, sing songs with nonsense words. She may turn into a regular entertainer.

It's at this stage, in our culture, that the messages boys and girls receive from adults become more obvious. For example, if a boy pulls books off a shelf, adults have a tendency to be indulgent—boys will be boys. The tone of their "no" says to the boy that exploration is important and they don't really expect him to follow rules all the time. If a girl does the same thing, the "no" is often less indulgent—this isn't ladylike, nice, or neat; the tone of voice conveys the message that good behavior is more important than exploration. What are the values you want for your child as she grows? If they are independence, curiosity, and friendliness, for example, then you can look for ways to develop these characteristics now.

The Tester likes the words "me" and "mine." She likes the idea that *she's the boss of herself,* the most important person in her world. She is very possessive of toys, her clothes, and even of objects that she decides to pick up and use. Her identification with things is intense—those that belong to her give her another way of defining herself. Since this is a natural tendency, and doesn't necessarily lead to becoming a "selfish" adult, it's important for you to understand her need to be possessive.

If she has her own cup and bowl, her own toy shelf, her own books, and even her own chair, corner, or area, your child will feel much more in control of everyday situations. This tendency to claim ownership, however, can cause problems if there are other children in the house or if she decides to lay claim to something not meant for her. You can avoid difficult situations if you help her to identify which toys are hers and which toys are to "share." In a house with more than one child, there will inevitably be conflicts. If you are consistent, however, in supporting her ("Yes, those are yours"), and in only asking her to share toys which you and she have labeled "sharing toys," the conflicts will be fewer. Your child may be friendly with

Your child needs things which are "hers" exclusively.

Inviting friends over to play will help your Tester learn how to share and communicate with children his own age.

other children, but she may also be threatened by them; she'll want to be the boss in her own house. You may find you need to keep a toy or two hidden away so that when other children visit they can have something to play with, too.

Your child may fuss endlessly when she's feeling insecure, or she may act clingy, like a much younger infant. She may scream when she's angry, or throw things, or refuse to talk to you. It takes a while to recognize what your child is feeling when she's being difficult. For example, if you're shelling peas with a friend, and your child keeps grabbing handfuls of peas and throwing them in the garbage, or throws them at you, or walks around the kitchen "singing" at the top of her lungs, or if she insists on sitting on your lap and squirming, what is she trying to say to you? She may not know. She may be angry because she feels left out; she may be bored; she may be showing off for your guest. Sometimes you can respond to her "message" successfully—by finding something interesting for her to do, by

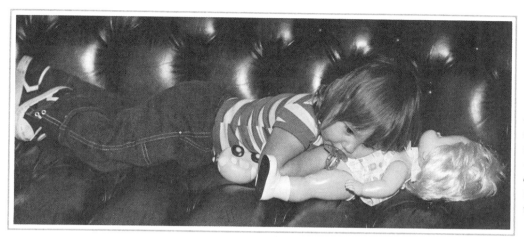

How your child acts during those times when she is less confident depends on her temperament and what is going on.

cuddling her, by letting her have some of her own peas to shell. At other times it may seem impossible to deal with her. Remember, this is a difficult time for your child, which makes it difficult for you; eventually she'll find less extreme ways to express herself.

Communication
Beginning to converse

The most dramatic change that takes place as your child goes through the Tester stage is that her language improves and expands and becomes more complex. It grows from simple naming of objects to use of short sentences, questions, and some real participation in conversations. Her

vocabulary is built upon what is familiar to her. She learns the names of her body parts and of her toys and of the people she knows. She learns to associate words with pictures. At this stage, when you read to your child, she may want to hear the same story over and over and participate by saying what's in the picture or repeating words she remembers from the story. Toward the end of the Tester stage, she might even be memorizing some of her simpler books and "reading" along with you from memory.

As is true of earlier stages, the child at the Tester stage will understand more than she can say. If you speak to her, ask her questions, or request that she do something, she can listen to what you are saying and often understand what you want. Actions, however, are still your child's primary way of understanding ideas. But now she might understand, for instance, "Do you want something to drink?" without needing to see a cup as a clue. Most children are delighted with this new understanding and want, naturally, to test it out. They love doing simple errands and being asked questions. As your child's ability to speak improves, she'll answer your questions with long involved "explanations" which may make very little sense to you. Speaking and being spoken to are enjoyable to her in themselves, before comprehension becomes fully a part of the process.

Adults communicate mostly with language, and don't need to constantly refer back to the objects or concrete situations they're discussing. But very small children need to see and experience firsthand the meaning of what's being talked about. Therefore, most discussions with your child at this stage should center around whatever is going on at the moment: what she sees, hears, feels, and smells; what she is doing and how it makes her feel.

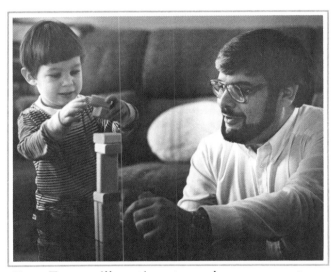

Your Tester will continue to need many concrete experiences to talk about with you.

The child is full of *whys,* and as in most things, she'll probably go overboard and ask "why" so frequently you'll wish you never heard the word. You'll have to figure out how many *whys* are aimed at getting more information, and how many are aimed at getting your goat; both kinds are inevitable forms of testing.

Many children at this stage are real jabberers. They talk when they are with you. They talk when they're playing next to other children. They even talk when they're alone. Some of this talk might be considered conversation, but most of it is trying out the rhythm of communication. Such talk can be fun in itself, and is great practice for the art of conversation. You don't need to worry about responding to everything your child says. As long as you're responsive, and as long as you include conversation in all your activities together, your child's language ability will get a healthy workout.

Behavior

Although your child is getting close to the age where he can understand "manners," he doesn't think in terms of neatness, efficiency, or politeness. Every situation he is involved in finds him testing, reacting, mastering. Rules that require him to consider his behavior are probably above his head.

Does this mean that you must accept all his behavior? Not at all. You will need, however, to consider each situation from your child's point of view. What does he want? How is he expressing this? Is it what he wants that goes against the grain, or is it what he's doing? This is a very important question for parents. Often the child will start some game, such as throwing his food, because he wants to play, or because he wants attention. It's not what he wants that is unacceptable to you, it's the food throwing. If you can find another game for him to play, or give him attention by eating with him (a bite for me, a bite for you), you may be able to stop what you don't like without giving him the idea that he is "bad."

One technique that clearly won't work is to ask the child, "How do you think that makes me feel?" He has no idea how it makes you feel. He is only beginning to understand that he has feelings, and that they can be affected by people and events. He sees your anger, frustration, and joy but has no idea that he can cause those feelings.

It is when the child enters this stage that you may begin to worry about his personality and character. Is he highly active? very fussy? Will he let adults talk without interrupting, or is he impossible to handle in public? Will he grow up to be a brat? Will he be a good person? To attempt to answer these questions definitively at this time is unfair to the child. He needs to *test* all kinds of behavior, not only to get your reaction but to see how it feels and to experience the consequences. He is growing and growth implies change. It's not within your power to know in advance the kind of person he will be. Better to ask, "What do I like about my child that I want to reinforce, that I believe will help him become the best he can be?"

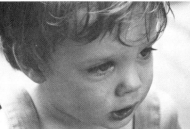

Understanding the World
New concepts and an expanding imagination

The Tester is coming to a new understanding of the world. She is forming concepts of how things work and what they are like. Her conclusions reflect her level of understanding, which in turn reflects her limited experience; therefore while her conclusions may satisfy *her,* they may be faulty from an adult's point of view. For example, unlike adults, who can see many aspects of an object and who can imagine it from many viewpoints, your child will think of an object in terms of one prominent feature. She'll compare two objects on the basis of only one quality; she may think that a tall thin glass holds more water than a short squat one because it's "higher."

A good way to help your child learn new concepts is to involve her in everyday tasks. When she puts objects away, she can put the big blocks on one side and the small blocks on another. She can learn to put puzzles on the top shelf and the trucks underneath. She can learn to tuck her dolls in with one blanket apiece. The language she uses may not match her level of understanding, though it will give you clues. For example, if you show her two boxes and ask her which is the large box and which is the small box, she can probably tell you; but if you bring in an even bigger box, she might say, "This is the big box, this is the big box, and this is the small box." Yet if you question her, she can tell you that the third box is bigger than the

second, and the second is bigger than the first. Watch for what your child actually *does* for signs of what she understands. Once you see what she understands, you can help her to use language appropriate to her ideas.

You won't always understand your child. It won't do you much good to argue with her, or say she's being silly if she makes no sense. Instead, figure out (if you can) just what it is she does think, and why. She doesn't understand that because of one thing another thing happens. For example, she understands that when you say, "Put on your jacket, it's cold outside," cold and jacket go together. What she doesn't understand is that she needs the jacket *because* it's cold. She may also understand things in relation to one another and not see them as separate things. If she's used to having a nap in the afternoon, for instance, she may think of naps and afternoons as being a part of the same thing. If she misses a nap one afternoon, she may insist it isn't afternoon yet; nap and afternoon are inseparable in her mind.

It is during the Tester stage that a child's imagination begins a rapid development. She learns that you can let one thing stand for another: a picture or a word can stand for an object; a block can even stand for a telephone. She might have a make-believe tea party and pretend to eat a piece of paper as if it were a piece of pie. She's beginning to think about and express thoughts about events she's not directly involved in. She might act out scenes she remembers—a fight she saw on TV, a horse galloping, the routine at her dinner table. But her thoughts are not always accurate or realistic by adult standards. She thinks that objects have intentions like people; if she trips on a chair, she might say the chair tried to hurt her. She's confused about where things come from: she may believe that trees and lakes and other natural phenomena are all made by people, and milk comes from cartons, not cows.

The child will want everything to be a game—going to the grocery store, taking a bath, making dinner. It's a good idea to make *some* of these times play times. For example, you could occasionally go window shopping, allowing her to take the lead.

Your child is gradually learning the meaning of "not now," but she doesn't really have a sense of duration. The famous question, "Is it time yet?" will come again and again. You might try using a sand timer or a timer that clicks off seconds and minutes to show her in a graphic way how long it will be until dinner, until it's time to clean up, until you can take her for a walk.

Because the Tester doesn't fully understand the concept of time, waiting may be difficult for him.

Relationships
Dealing with complex emotions

On a good day, your child's wish to *do things herself* can seem like a blessing. She'll run little errands for you, help you with your work, put her own toys away, help you hold the baby while you give him a bath. On bad days, this same trait can become a curse. She may want to help you shop, or put all your carefully arranged papers away, or dress herself when

you're in a hurry. On a normal day, you may have to wait very patiently while she tries to accomplish something, such as putting on a jacket, and you'll have to balance your desire to help against her desire to achieve.

Your relationship will become more complex. By now your child is familiar with what happens at mealtime, what happens when other family members get home, what happens when it's naptime or bedtime. Although she'll want to test these situations by stalling or starting games at inconvenient times, you can head her off by taking advantage of her knowledge. You might start five minutes before naptime and say: "Do you know what happens after we play in the afternoon?" ("Naptime.") "That's right. And if you want to look at these two books for a few minutes you can choose which one I'll read to you." This

gives her a way to make the transition to naptime with an idea in her head of what will happen. It gives her a sense of control.

If you're trying to finish cooking dinner, and your child wants to play, it's perfectly reasonable to say, "Jessie, I need to do this now." If she's restless, you can take a minute to help her find something to play with. If she wants to do something with you, you can let her know that now is not the time for you to play, but that she can be nearby.

Be sure that your expectations are reasonable. If, for example, you go to a neighbor's house and there are no other children to play with, it's not very realistic to expect your child to sit quietly with no toys. It *is* reasonable to help her choose two or three quiet toys ahead of time and then during the visit ask her to play with them while you talk with your neighbor.

A large part of good discipline is timing. If you ask a child to come take her nap when she's in the middle of a fascinating game, she'll probably put up a fuss. Instead, help her wind the game down, or suggest a transitional activity, such as going for a short walk.

Try to be aware of your child's energy level. If she's very excited, chances are she won't want to be crossed; she may need some quiet game to help her calm down. If she's tired, it will be difficult to ask her to do anything.

Tantrums may be frequent at this stage. A tantrum can mean screaming, slapping, lashing out wildly, refusing to budge, or beating the floor and crying uncontrollably. Many parents either scream back or try to reason. Neither of these "tactics" works. Instead, try to stay as calm as possible, and try to calm your child: rock her, hold her, rub her back. Sometimes it helps to suggest some activity: "Let's go outside for a walk" or "Let's do some exercises." Sometimes she just needs to be left alone.

The first thing in dealing with a screaming child is not to resolve the argument; it is to calm her down. Don't let your child get her way by screaming. If she thinks that screaming will get her what she wants, she'll make a habit of it. Hitting or threatening to hit the child will frighten her and make her more tense and unhappy; it also won't teach her anything about finding ways to ask for what she wants without a tantrum.

One major help you can give your child is to acknowledge and attach language to her feelings

Emotions are inside a child, but they are affected by what happens around her. When trying to understand your child's emotions, pay close attention to what's really going on. Is she angry, frustrated, tired? You might ask her to talk about how she feels or what she wants. Is she anxious, lonely? Let her know you understand how she feels. You might say: "You sure had a rough time this morning, didn't you? You were really angry at me. I'm glad you're feeling better now." While the child might not understand all the words, especially early in this stage, she *will* understand your tone and concern. "Punishing" the child by acting angry or cold is not helpful. She may think you are rejecting her, not just reacting to something she's done.

It's also good to tell the child how *you* feel. "I was angry that you screamed in the grocery store." Let her know exactly what she did that annoyed you. What you want to communicate is that you're annoyed by what she's *done,* not by who she *is*; she may have done something "bad," but she's not a bad person. Listen to your voice when you tell her how you feel; your tone of voice and body language communicate even more than your words.

In some families, sibling rivalry becomes a problem. It's especially difficult if there's a new baby stealing your attention, or if there's a Creeper-Crawler who grabs a Tester's toys. You can help your child find ways to join you when you're caring for another child, or help her get involved with something special of her own. You may have to be a toy referee, helping each child in the household learn whose toys belong to whom. Your child might appreciate a box or closet to keep her toys in so other children can't get at them without her permission.

Often the child is perfectly content to play alone—she has so much to do! She enjoys showing you what she is doing. When there's company, however, she may be more interested in showing off, or she may feel invaded and throw a fit if anyone tries to touch something that's hers. You can avoid some of this behavior by making sure she understands what is expected of her and what she can expect. If company is coming she might be allowed to stay up until they arrive, with the understanding that she will go to bed shortly thereafter. If another child is coming to visit, let her choose two or three toys to share with the child. A large part of helping your child handle social situations is thinking ahead and helping her get an idea of what her choices are.

You have been living with a growing, changing, challenging child for three years. You've given her the support, attention, encouragement, and affection that form the groundwork for further growth. You've helped her learn many things about the physical and social world and have taught her many of the skills she will need to become an active, productive person. She has probably taught *you* many things—patience for one, and an appreciation of the uniqueness of each human life. You have experienced feelings of elation, joy, sorrow, frustration, love, anger, wonder. We hope that through it all you have come to recognize your expertise as a parent, and that you will continue to develop your skills and share them with others. May you continue to grow and learn, together with your child.

Things to Do

Play Ball!

Playing ball now becomes more elaborate, both in terms of the variety of balls that can be used and in terms of what the child will be able to do with them (with your help). Balls can come in all shapes and sizes; bean bags, yarn balls, small rubber balls, large beach balls, Nerf balls, and balloons. Encourage the child to throw them at a target (a trash can, a box with a hole cut in it, a tree). Show her how to kick a ball back and forth or along a pathway you have created, around obstacles, or into a box. There are many, many ways to "play ball" that are challenging and fun for both of you and that help the child gain greater control of her body.

Water Play and Pouring for Active Learning

Find a place where you feel comfortable with water being splashed—outside if the weather permits. Fill a large pan with water and give your child a funnel and containers for pouring (measuring cups and spoons, a sieve, bottles of various sizes and shapes, an egg beater. Then let her go at it! Add some dishwashing liquid to create bubbles. While she's playing in the water, give your child some objects that float and others that sink (buttons, bottlecaps, paperclips, soap, a clothespin, small wooden objects, a tightly closed plastic bottle).

Have the child experiment with objects and then sort them into two piles according to whether they float or sink. You can also give your child sand, rice, or grits for pouring. For exploration, provide funnels, small jars, and bottles of different sizes and shapes.

What Happens Next?

Make a personalized activity book for the child. Take pictures of her doing everyday things: eating breakfast, getting dressed, bathing, at her day care, playing with toys, taking a nap, reading with someone, playing with others. Mount the pictures on heavy cardboard and describe each picture with a simple sentence that tells what the child is doing. Put the pictures in the order in which they generally occur during the day. When going through the book with the child, ask "What happens next?" to see if she can anticipate the events in her day.

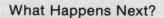

Up and Over and Under

Create an obstacle course that requires the child to climb over, crawl through or under, jump across, run around, etc. Join in if you want! She will be delighted that she can crawl under some things much better than you can. Encourage her to add different "obstacles" to the course.

Filling in the Blanks

When reading stories that are familiar to your child, leave out some of the key words as you go along. Encourage the child to "fill in the blanks." As you repeat this activity, she may try to fill in more and more of the story, until at last she may well "read" you the whole story!

Can You . . . ?

Your child's understanding of words has increased enormously by the Tester stage. One fun way to find out just what the child understands is to play a game similar to "Simon Says." Simply ask her, "Can you put your hands on your head? touch the ground? walk on tiptoe? hop? jump? do a somersault? touch your knees? walk backwards?"

When you first play this game, you may want to join in the different activities. Then, if the child is unsure of the words, she can mimic your actions. When she seems to understand the words, you can stop participating. You can add greater complexity to the game later on by asking the child to do two things in a sequence, such as "jump and then touch the ground" or "turn around and touch your toes."

Appendix
Other Resources

Troubles and Triumphs at Home

Troubles and Triumphs at Home is a set of four sound filmstrips and four booklets for parents of preschool children with special needs. In parents' own words, the filmstrips offer strategies for dealing with behavior problems and contributing to children's learning and language development. The purpose is to encourage parents to objectively analyze their own childrearing practices and to develop creative, developmentally appropriate solutions to problems they find in maintaining normal family functioning. Instead of offering pat solutions, the materials present some general problem-solving approaches and show examples of how certain families have applied these approaches in their own homes.

The filmstrips are designed to be used in group settings. Each package contains both Spanish and English versions of the soundtracks and parent booklets and a parent meeting guide for the leader of the group.

Titles in the Series:

When "I've Told You a Thousand Times" Isn't Enough. Three important strategies parents can use to minimize many child behavior problems.

Converting Conflict to Calm. How parents can restructure problem situations to meet their own needs for order and calm, while meeting their preschool children's needs for active involvement with the world around them.

Let Them Do It. How parents can encourage self-reliance and the development of mental and physical skills by giving children simple household responsibilities.

Let Them Say It. Why language learning is a natural part of any activity and how parents can incorporate oral or sign communication into common daily activities such as bathing, cooking, dressing, cleaning.

The four accompanying parent booklets contain additional tips and information for parents. They are designed for photocopying, so additional copies can be made for group sessions. The parent meeting guide contains suggestions for organizing parent support meetings and structuring group activities around each of the four topics.

Young Children in Action

Young Children in Action is a comprehensive resource for adults who work with preschool children. More than a source-book for activities, this 336-page guide provides a description of the Cognitively Oriented Curriculum, a tested and demonstrated program in use since 1962. The curriculum is based on the developmental theory of Jean Piaget: "the most complete and coherent theory available." The curriculum framework outlined in the book has been used with the full range of preschool children, including mildly to severely handicapped, economically disadvantaged and gifted children as well as middle class, urban, and rural children in the U.S., Australia and Latin America.

The book is organized into two parts supplemented by appendices. Part One deals with "The Classroom, the Day, the Staff." These chapters outline the history of the curriculum, the organization of the daily routine, room arrangement principles, team planning and team teaching.

Part Two, "Key Experiences for Cognitive Development," describes how key experiences derived from developmental theory serve as the content or the "heart" of the curriculum. The 50 key experiences are tools to help teachers recognize basic intellectual processes and extend and enrich classroom activities.

Young Children in Action is well illustrated with both photographs and sketches. Each chapter includes suggestions for related films and readings. The appendices include a summary of teaching methods, curriculum checklists, observation records, a parent interview form and an assessment record. Those seeking to understand why as well as how to implement child development ideas will find **Young Children in Action** an invaluable guide.

Your Baby's Day: A Time for Learning

Your Baby's Day: A Time for Learning is a new filmstrip/audio cassette production from The High/Scope Press which demonstrates ways to enhance infant development through routine activities—feeding, changing, bathing, etc. Designed to make parents and other caregivers aware of their important role in a child's development at three important stages: newborn; four to eight months; and eight months to a year. Useful for parents-to-be, hospital training programs, high school and community college courses in child development, or for training adults in day care centers. Realistic, supportive suggestions for adult-infant interactions. Print guide included.

For price and order information, contact:

The High/Scope Press
600 North River St., Ypsilanti, Michigan 48197
(313) 485-2000

References

Brazelton, T. Berry. *Becoming a Family.* New York: Dell Publishing Co., Inc., 1980.

Brazelton. T. Berry. *Infants and Mothers: Differences in Development.* New York: Dell Publishing Co., Inc., 1969.

Brazelton, T. Berry. *Toddlers and Parents: A Declaration of Independence.* New York: Dell Publishing Co., Inc., 1974.

Bruner, J., M. Cole, and B. Lloyd, eds. *The Developing Child Series.* Cambridge, MA: Harvard University Press, 1977.

Kagan, J., R.B Kearsley, and P.R. Zelazo. *Infancy: Its Place in Human Development.* Cambridge, MA: Harvard University Press, 1978.

Lewis, M., and L.A. Rosenblum, eds. *The Development of Affect.* New York: Plenum Press, 1978.

Lewis, M., and L.A. Rosenblum. *The Effect of the Infant on the Caregiver.* New York: John Wiley & Sons, 1974.

Osofsky, J.O., ed. *Handbook of Infant Development.* New York: John Wiley & Sons, 1979.

Pearce, J.C. *Magical Child: Rediscovering Nature's Plan for Our Children.* New York: E.P. Dutton, 1977.

Piaget, J. *The Origins of Intelligence in Children.* New York: W.W. Norton Company, Inc., 1952.

Rozdilsky, M., and B. Banet, *What Now? A Handbook for New Parents.* New York: Charles Scribner's Sons, 1972.

Uzgiris, I.C., and J. McV. Hunt. *Assessment in Infancy: Ordinal Scales of Psychological Development.* Chicago: University of Illinois Press, 1975.

White, Burton L. *The First Three Years of Life.* New York: Avon, 1975.

Index

Environment: impact on parent, 15; impact on infant, 15

Equipment, infant: infant seat, 28; car seat, 62; choosing, 62-63; jump seat, 62-63; playpen, 62; food mill, 68

Events: infant's anticipation of, 45

Exercise: during diapering, 20-21; for the newborn, 28; need for, 145

Experimenter: your child as, 104

Experts: opinions of, 6

Explanations: use of to foster speech, 128

Exploration: through gazing, 44, 49; value of, 47-49; through grasping, 61, 83; intentional, 82; what happens if . . ., 85; experimentation as, 104; problem-solving as, 125-126; from curiosity, 142; testing as, 144; through language, 156. *See also* Babbling, Communication, Feeding, Language, Problem-solving

Father. *See* Caregiver, Parenting

Fear: of heights, 87; falling, 87

Feeding: questions about, 18; place for, 18; positions for, 18; sibling reactions to, 18; schedules for, 18-19; patterns of, 19; problems with, 19; distractions during, 19, 68; reactions of infant to your mood, 19; nourishment, 19; introducing a spoon, 68; introducing solids, 68; finger foods, 68-69; self, 69, 122; fostering independence, 146; acceptable behavior in self-feeding, 157. *See also* Eating

Feelings: initial reactions to having a baby, 15; indication of child's, 90; a child's understanding of, 157. *See also* Emotions

Feet: infant's discovery of, 58

Focus: infant's ability to, 17; infant's control of focusing, 36

Food: infant's exploration of, 68; allowing child to make choices, 148; introducing new, 149. *See also* Eating, Feeding

Frustration: causes of in infant, 58, 92; indicators of infant's, 89, 92; related to need for independence, 141

Games: peek-a-boo, 50, 66, 73, 86, 125; value of accidental, 59, 90; child's initiation of, 63, 125; use of mirror for, 65-66, 125; roughhousing, 65, 113; hide-and-seek, 68; setting limits on, 84; during daily activities, 91, 159; introducing to child, 103

Gazing: value of, 44; role in exploration, 47-49

Goals: child's ability to develop complex, 134. *See also* Concepts

Goal-setting: the infant's ability to do, 82-83, 85

Growth: spurts, 83. *See also* Development

Guilt: causes of in parent, 26

Hands: infant's discovery of, 47; bringing to mouth, 48; exploring with, 64; controlled use of in toddler, 149

Head: support of, 37, 46-47

Hearing: activities to develop infant's, 45; coordination with vision, 45

Humor: infant's sense of, 90; developing sense of in toddler, 153

Observations: guided, 5; knowledge gained about child by, 7; recording in a diary, 7; by child, 125

Observer: your role as, 6, 103

Overstimulation: infant's reactions to, 36; causes of, 51-52; cues indicating, 52; response to, 52

Pacifiers, 25

Parenting: definition of, 4; supports for, 4; adjusting to, 4; questions to consider, 4; developing skills of, 4-5; your changing needs, 66-67; dealing with your emotions, 93

Pat-a-cake, 108

Patience: an infant's learning of, 92; finding your limits, 111; during toilet training, 123; when the child tests your, 141-142

Peek-a-boo, 50, 66, 73, 86, 125

Penis: discovery of, 64-65, 83

Personality: elements of, 7; indications of at birth, 14; the infant's developing, 22-23; as related to learning, 78; observing the child's, 157. *See also* Temperament

Piaget, Jean, ix, 168

Plan: child's mental ability to, 85-86

Planning: this book as a resource for, 6-7

Play: water, 65; the value of solitary, 113; with other children, 127; supporting your child's, 132; importance of for toddler, 150-151; your role in your toddler's, 150-151

Pleasure: infant's indications of, 23, 46

Poisons: common household, 88

Praise, value of, 130

Predictability: indicators of infant's, 41

Preferences: indicators of infant's, 41-42; development of in infant, 49

Problem-solving: using this book as a resource for, 6; understanding how things work, 125-126, 144, 149. *See also* Objects, "Why?"

Rattles, 61

Reaching: motivation for, 72

Recognition: of primary caregiver, 22. *See also* Name, Responses

Reflexes: rooting, 16; grasping, 16; sucking, 16; turning head, 17; smile, 17

Repetition: of infant's sounds, 70; of actions by infant, 73. *See also* Imitation, Learning

Responses: watching for in infant, 14; types of infant, 42; importance of parent's, 49; of infant to recognized and strange objects/people, 50

Rhythms: responding to speech, 17, 22; as technique for soothing infant, 24

Rocking, 3

Role play: beginning of, 87; definition of, 131; value of, 131. *See also* Imagination, Imitation

Rolling over, 58-59

Routine: hospital, 10, 12, 15; time together, 51; for transition times, 91; establishing a daily, 107; importance of maintaining, 135. *See also* Limits, Schedule

Temperament: an infant's, 7, 21, 24, 37; indications of, 12, 89; definition and description of, 39-43. *See also* Character, Personality

Temperature: infant responses to changes in, 42

Thinking: signs of in infant, 86; early thinking and reasoning, 106. *See also* Concepts

Threats: use of, 135, 137. *See also* Discipline

Thumbsucking, 25-26

Time: infant's understanding of, 86; toddler's understanding of, 138

Toilet training: beginnings of, 123; guidelines for, 146

Touch: value of, 17; as a means of communication, 31. *See also* Communication

Toys: crib, 49; using household objects as, 61, 102, 150; guidelines for choosing, 71; learning how they work, 125-126; supporting play with, 132; how toddlers "share," 153-154. *See also* Equipment

Transition times: effect on infant's moods, 42; activities/preparations for, 91; techniques to make them smoothe, 160-161. *See also* Routine, Schedule

Trust: developing infant's, 20, 22-23, 63; establishing relationship with infant, 93. *See also* Security

Vagina: discovery of, 83

Vision: range of infant's, 17, 29, 31, 35; coordination with hearing, 44-45

Vocabulary-building: through giving reasons, 109; providing descriptions, 109; praise, 109; questions, 109; providing information, 109. *See also* Communication, Language

"Wait": understanding the concept, 136; learning to, 151; learning the meaning of "not now," 159

Walk: learning to, 100. *See also* "Cruising"

Weaning: meaning for child, 90; dealing with your feelings about, 93

"Why?": the importance of to child's learning, 144; child's use of, 156. *See also* Problem-solving

Words: associated with events and things, 109; linked with action, 109, 128; increased understanding of, 128. *See also* Language

Notes